NOTES FROM THE HARD SHOULDER

NOTES FROM THE HARD SHOULDER

James May

This paperback edition first published in Great Britain in
2007 by
Virgin Books Ltd
Thames Wharf Studios
Rainville Road
London
W6 9HA

A catalogue record for this book is available from
the British Library.

ISBN 978 0 7535 1202 9

The paper used in this book is a natural, recyclable product
made from wood grown in sustainable forests. The
manufacturing process conforms to the regulations of the
country of origin.

Typeset by TW Typesetting, Plymouth, Devon
Printed in the UK by CPI Bookmarque, Croydon, CR0 4TD

To Pullin and Green, for the opportunity

CONTENTS

PART 1 – I'VE A GOOD MIND TO WRITE A LETTER

PLEASE KEEP OFF THE MUD

It is time, now that someone has raised the truly preposterous notion of congestion charging in our national parks, to acknowledge a few painful realities about the countryside. There is a feeling at large that cars somehow do not belong in the countryside; I now put it to you that in fact the countryside belongs to the car.

Before anyone writes in with a volume of Rupert Brooke, I should make it clear that I understand perfectly the position occupied by the rural idyll in the English national consciousness; how its gently swaying fields of corn are instantly evoked by thoughts of home when abroad; how the memory of England endures not as a shopping centre or theme park but as an endless Arcadian vista who gave her flowers to love etc. But how are we to enjoy all this, if not from the car?

You could go for a walk, say some, but have you seen the size of the place? It would take me two days to reach the edge of it from where I live, and even then there would be a few golf courses to negotiate before I arrived in the other Eden. Cycling? Civilised bicycles only work on the road, and the road is only there because of cars. If you try off-roading on one of these so-called 'mountain' bikes, farmers will shoot at you. And I have to say that if I were a farmer, and you rode across my field with an inverted polystyrene fruit bowl on your head astride £2,000-worth of unobtanium, I'd shoot at you as well.

No – the problem is not that people keep driving through the countryside, it's that people keep living there.

If you're a farmer, tilling manfully on the land to produce the things I love to eat, then that's fine. Likewise a gamekeeper or some old toff, since they're not safe in the city. Also fine is running a country pub, as that's where I like to stop for a pie. But the rest of you – and especially those of you who think a two-inch-high ribbon of tarmac is somehow 'ruining the countryside' – can bugger off, because your houses are spoiling the view from my Porsche.

If, for example, you're a merchant banker working in the City, you should live in the City near the bank. If you're the manager of a country bank, you should live in the flat above it or in a windowless bothy alongside. Similarly, working for a software consultancy and living in the sticks is as absurd as turning up for work at a software consultancy in a straw hat singing ee-aye-ee-aye-oh. I don't want to escape to the countryside in my car to be rewarded with an endless rolling panorama of Barratt Homes. It's the ruin of England.

Everyone I know who lives in the cuds is, in terms of their demands, aspirations and general lifestyle, exactly the same as my neighbours in London. They are separated from me by nothing more than a very, very big garden. They drive into the town every day and complain about congestion, without stopping to think for long enough to realise that the road isn't there so that they can come in, it's there so I can get out in something with a flat six and enjoy a world as Adam would have known it.

The harsh truth is that cod country living is a privilege bequeathed entirely by the roads and motor transport. So if you live in Chodford and despise all things automotive, you should live as I imagine country folk did before the car was invented. That is, like a chicken; in your own poo, driven mad by blight and at the mercy of wild animals. You should ride a donkey, and the road to your damp dwelling should be a rough track beset by bandits and deranged inbreds with huge hands and one eye in the middle of their faces.

Actually, I'd go further than that. You should not be allowed anything in life that is in any way dependent on road transport. So no fresh shiitake mushrooms from the charming deli in the village, because they arrived in a van. You'll have to bake your own bread in the little cubby holes at the side of your Aga – the ones with the red-hot handles. And no reading the *Daily Telegraph*, because it isn't really a telegraph at all. It comes in a van as well.

Anti-car sentiment is nowhere as incongruous as it is in the countryside. In fact, the beauty of the countryside in modern times is that you can drive through it, look at it and then leave it alone. Its principal function is for the growing of carrots, but after that, it's what sports cars were invented for.

THIS JAGUAR LOOKS A BIT HALF-BAKED TO ME

I've now been sitting here for some hours looking at a picture of the Jaguar X-Type estate fitted with the maker's optional 'Sports Collection' body styling package. And I have to say, I'm just not sure about it.

To explain why, we have to go back a few weeks to an idle evening when I decided that I would make a Chinese meal. And I don't mean one contrived from a packet sauce and a tin of water chestnuts. I mean the real thing, like that bloke Ken Whatsit would do.

Now, I don't really rate myself as a chef. Anything outside the orbit of the old school favourites – shepherd's pie, cheesy pasta – is frankly a bit of a mystery. But that doesn't matter, because you can buy sets of instructions for clever cooking and the picture on the front is usually so good it's tempting just to eat the book.

I did everything properly. I went to a Chinese supermarket for the ingredients and I borrowed a wok from a neighbour. The preparation time amounted to many hours of careful chopping and straining.

But then it started to go wrong. I've heard a theory that oriental cooking is the way it is because of a historical shortage of fuel, so everything is cut up small and it's all cooked together in one very thin utensil that becomes blindingly hot in seconds. It all happened far too quickly.

I think the word that best sums up my Szechuan double-cooked pork with chow mein is 'grey'.

Undeterred, I decided to try an Indian instead, since the cooking process would then be much more leisurely. I visited a proper Indian food shop and started from scratch with raw spices, ghee, basmati rice and what have you. I ground, roasted, made pastes, marinated things overnight – in fact, my chicken tikka bhuna with peas pilau took almost two days to complete. It could best be described as 'brown'.

As a result of all this I have decided to abandon any ridiculous pretence of being multi-culti and acknowledge that if I fancy a Chinese or an Indian, I'll find some Chinese or Indian people to make it for me. There are several within a few hundred paces of my house, as it happens, and they are much, much better at this sort of thing than I am because they are steeped in the appropriate culture and traditions; rather in the way that I know, almost instinctively, what to do with Spam.

Similarly, I may have spent many hours as a boy sketching supercars in the back of my geometry exercise book with my Oxford Mathematical Instruments set, but I will still recognise that real car designers are better. So if I buy a car that I think looks good, I'll leave it alone. I don't order a butter chicken from the Light of Nepal and then start adding some extra ingredients I brought along from home.

In fairness to Jaguar, the 'Sports Collection' body package is the work of the factory, so presumably all the bits will fit properly. But I can't help wondering why, if it looks so good, they don't just make it like that in the first place. And in what other arena of sporting endeavour is weight added for no performance gain? This is like an Olympic sprinter thinking he'd be better off if he was a bit fatter.

Car manufacturers are developing an unhealthy appetite for mucking about with things that were already right. I've just driven a new and extra-sporty version of the Audi TT, which has a harder suspension, ridiculous bucket seats that feel like, well, buckets, daft alloy wheels that stick out further than the tyres and which you will kerb on the way home from the showroom and, worst of all, a black roof. They've completely ruined it. It was a seminal and much-trumpeted bit of automotive design, but somebody imagined it could be improved with a tin of Humbrol enamel. Even the Subaru Impreza Turbo, which comes sort of pre-kitted, looks better left alone.

I know the modified-car scene is a huge and vibrant one. I've examined the work of the lads who are into it and a lot of it is really exquisitely done and bought at the expense of still living at home with mum. Good for them. But I still don't believe I've ever seen a modified Citroen Saxo or Vauxhall Corsa that looked better than the ones Citroen and Vauxhall came up with.

So here's a tip. If you open the fridge tonight and find that it contains, like mine, a pork chop, some potatoes and a sprig of broccoli, have pork chop with potatoes and broccoli for dinner.

BRITAIN'S SURFACE INDUSTRY FAILS TO DELIVER

Last year, the main road that runs perpendicular to the little road I live on was resurfaced. And I know what you're expecting me to say next.

That it's now worse than it ever was, is covered in nasty grit that destroys underseal, and has already been dug up by the GPO to lay some new telephone cables. But no. This was by far the most professional, efficient and well-managed civil engineering project I've ever witnessed at close quarters.

The work began at around 10 o'clock one night, when all the traffic had died down. The whole road was closed, and an army of stout men turned up with a gigantic fire-belching engine, a sort of mechanical version of that Norwegian cheese slicer, the one that you use to put parmesan shavings on the top of your salad if people are coming round for dinner.

This thing, moving at a speed so imperceptible that in the time it took me to drink three pints and have a game of darts it had travelled only about 30 yards, removed exactly three inches from the top of the road surface while somehow avoiding the drains and man-hole covers. Once the pub had shut, and because I had no one left to talk to, I went to watch the miracle unfold and have a ride on the iron horse.

The next morning, just before the rush-hour started, the bollards, the security tape, the cheese slicer and the workers' tea tent thing were all removed and the road was opened again. It wasn't very good, because each manhole cover now assumed the proportions of Ayers Rock and the grooves left by the skimming machine tended to steer one's motorcycle into the path of oncoming traffic. But it was open.

The next night, it was closed again. Now another roaring inferno worthy of Hieronymus Bosch himself turned up to lay the new surface, inching along the street and dispensing the gleaming, sweet-smelling blacktop of hope in its wake. By morning it was finished, and this little corner of UK PLC was back in business, thanks largely to some blokes from Poland.

And the results were – and there really is no other word for this – perfect. People were on their hands and knees at the kerb examining the road and searching vainly for flaws. Small children were riding up and down on bicycles, marvelling at its smoothness. People in shops could be heard saying, 'Have you driven on the new road yet?' There had not been such a collective sense of wonderment since the invention of radio.

Even now, a year on, I can find only two small patches that have been disturbed, and these have been mended almost invisibly. It really is a pleasure to arrive home by car.

So can someone explain the appalling Horlicks that's been made of the side road running parallel to mine? It was closed and excavated for the purposes of installing a new water main, although for the most part it was simply closed. The job is now complete, and in fairness the contractor has made good the road, in the sense that I don't actually fall down a hole when I'm making my way home from the pub at night. But, God in heaven, it's unsightly. The new tarmac is the wrong colour, the wrong texture, and it isn't flush with the old stuff.

How can I portray the sheer horror of these road repairs? Let me put it this way. If one of the perfectly laid green tiles from my bathroom floor was broken, this lot would come around, affix a slightly smaller brown tile of half the thickness, fill in the gaps with the wrong colour grout and then stand back and say, 'Yep, that looks pretty good.'

It's not even an isolated case. Since noting this, I have been walking around with my head bowed, ignoring the cheery greetings of my neighbours, totally absorbed in studying the road surface. Everywhere I look it's a patchwork of cack-handed repairs completed so shoddily that it's a mystery the place isn't littered with spilled bicyclists. Why is this? It can't be any harder or more expensive to repair a road properly than it is to do it badly.

Tadek, Jarek and Marik have shown that first-class road repairs are possible in Britain. Yet, for some reason, we don't seem to think it matters beyond the main thoroughfares. The people around here studiously mend their window frames, grow brightly coloured shrubs and flowers in their front gardens and paint their front doors in amusing colours. Yet this model of English urban splendour faces a road that appears to have been imported from 1990s Bosnia.

The side roads of England are a disgrace. Can somebody please explain why?

MY CUP RUNNETH OVER AND INTO THE CENTRE CONSOLE

Some time ago, the national press published the findings of a report in which continental Europeans denounced the British as 'a nation of coffee philistines'.

An important point was missed in all this. We are not coffee philistines at all; we have become philistines because of coffee. There is now barely a corner of a British high street that hasn't been commandeered by a bean-bashing multinational of some kind, and within them can be found people talking in a strange and subversive code. You'd be forgiven for wondering how the nation had survived until now without a regular double skinny latte mocha choca top before work.

For confirmation of this, look no further than our obsession with in-car cup holders. Over its brief history, the cup holder as found in European and Japanese cars has evolved from a token fixture intended to persuade Americans to buy the car (US sales of the Jaguar XJ once suffered for the car's want of one) to a device of such cunning and complexity that it can embody more engineering and design expertise than once went into a whole vehicle. And yet the only thing that will fit safely into a cup holder is a cardboard cup from a coffee-shop chain.

Meanwhile, tea – the drink that made Britain great – has been virtually forgotten. Tea is the sustainer of honest toil and remains the second most important commodity of the British building trade after sugar. Some historians believe that the mildly medicinal quality of tea actually encouraged industrialisation, because it allowed our manufacturing centres to proliferate quicker than the bowel disorders that would otherwise have destroyed their populations. Apart from anything else, a Frenchman or Italian, fuelled by espresso that could be used to build roads, would have been far too jittery to sit down patiently and invent the steam engine or the flying shuttle.

Of course, a nominal cup of tea can be bought from Cafe Nation or Buckstars or whatever these left-wing chattering houses are called, but it is a dismal offering in which bag, tepid water and milk have all been introduced to the vessel simultaneously. Furthermore, tea cannot really be enjoyed out of cardboard. It should be served in a chipped ceramic mug (if engaged in something manly, such as roofing or restoring an old sports car) or a bone china cup and saucer (if there is any risk, however slight, of a visit from your mother). Curiously, neither of these things will fit in a car's cup holder.

The cup holder, then, can be regarded at best as the perpetrator of a dangerous fad; at worst as the cradle of the enemies of Britishness.

The problem becomes even more acute if you fancy a proper drink. The instant I joined Salim Khoury at the *Telegraph* Motor Show, I sensed that he would go home a disappointed man. We had come to test the versatility of cup holders.

Khoury is manager of the American Bar at The Savoy, where he has worked since 1969. He came to Britain from his native Beirut, where he learned the subtleties of cocktail making in response to the demands of a then enormous American hotel clientele.

Yet despite the predominantly American image of drinks such as the Manhattan and the Cosmopolitan, he maintains that 'Britain really comes top of the world in cocktails; in making them and in creating them.' His most recent invention is the Telesuite, a new cocktail to celebrate the inauguration of the Savoy's electronic virtual-conferencing arrangement with New York's Waldorf Astoria. The ingredients include absinthe, which is known to be conducive to brainstorming.

Khoury comes equipped as a sort of roving international ambassador of correct cocktail etiquette. His briefcase is a beautiful wood-inlaid aluminium job divided into foam-lined compartments for measuring jug, log-handled stirring spoon, fruit knife, ice bucket, a strainer for taking the pith, ice tongs, a champagne stopper and, of course, the silver shaker itself. 'I stir my Martinis. I never shake,' he says, in response to the inevitable comparison with Bond.

He also brings a selection of glasses, some of them traditional, such as the typical champagne flute, and some of them the trademarks of his bar, such as the Savoy's own more generous champagne goblet, the Martini glass that has been an unassailable feature of the hotel since the '20s, and a huge cut-glass balloon suitable for cognac – a particular favourite of Churchill, apparently.

Sadly, none of them fit in a cup holder.

Cup holders can be divided into two basic types. There is the first phase of development, where they took the simple form of a tapered cup-shaped hollow somewhere on the facia, there to satisfy the supposed demand for cup holders at minimum expense. The most pathetic example of Phase One cup holders probably occurred on a Seat Arosa I once owned, in which the inside of the glovebox lid boasted two vague circular indentations. They were little more than a desperate grasp at cup-holder credibility, a sort of visual indication to Place Cups Here, nothing more. But that was in the mid-'90s, a time when it was suddenly believed that not having a cup holder was like admitting to still having drum brakes at the front.

Phase One cup holders still survive on plenty of cars and are at least suitable for storing mobile phones. They might even accept the base of a champagne flute or wine glass, but a lot depends on location. In the VW Beetle, for example, the diameter of the cup holes is slightly smaller than that of the base of Khoury's Martini glass, and in any case the Martini would have to be tipped on to its side in order to clear the bottom of the dashboard's central binnacle before final insertion. The only drink that can safely be turned on its side is one with a lid on it, which immediately puts us back in the hands of Cafe Nero.

The service is rather better on the Rolls-Royce stand, and especially in the rear of the Phantom, which is a good venue for a drink. Here, the cup-holder tray – essentially still a Phase One type – extends from beneath the seat and will at least accept the pint pot Khoury brought along at my personal insistence (pints not actually being available in the American Bar), since it has sufficient headroom. Rolls-Royce will also supply a proper drinks cabinet, complete with glasses, if desired. But at £240,000 one has to wonder why it isn't standard. You can find a mini bar in a £50 hotel room these days.

Phase Two cup holders are much more fatuous. These are the spring-loaded, extending and retracting type that testify to cup-holder oneupmanship on the part of car manufacturers. Once the novelty of simply having a cup holder wore off – and that happened pretty quickly – it became important for car owners to be able to impress passengers with cup-holder complexity. Top speeds and 0–60mph times have clearly been usurped by the number of stages in your cup holder's deployment. Some of them emerge like time-lapsed film of a daffodil opening, or expand into a sort of plastic balletic first position.

Especially idiotic examples of Phase Two cup holders – but there are many more – occur in the new BMW 5-Series and the Saab 9-3. In the BMW, the central holder not only sprouts from the dashboard, it actually follows a curved path towards the driving seat, as if reaching an extra inch or two for your cappuccino grande might be too much effort.

But Saab can beat that. Its offering is so geometrically baffling that it stands as a testimony to the lifetime's work of Euclid. And you thought the electric hood was clever. The whole assembly collapses into a slot no broader than a disposable biro and is, in purely mechanical terms, a brilliant achievement.

But for what? Khoury's Cosmopolitan, a fine drink in which 'flavour is more important than alcoholic content, absolutely', will either fall out or snap the device clean off. In the BMW, the base of the White Lady glass can be coaxed past the sprung lip intended to hold your king-size Americano in check, but then, because the lip is like a barb, cannot be extracted unless it is turned on its side. It can't be turned on its side until the contents have been drunk. We are now in a cup-holder Catch 22 situation, and the only answer seems to be to turn the car upside down and empty the peerless beverage into a bucket.

This whole cup-holder thing really hasn't been thought through properly. All credit is due to Citroen, then, for maintaining, with the Pluriel, an immutable that was established with the Mini – namely, that the door pockets should be broad enough to accommodate a wine bottle. But for the glasses? Nothing.

There are two conclusions to be drawn from this impromptu investigation into cup holders. The first is that the amount of wit and ingenuity being discharged in the design of them is out of all proportion to the import of their function. There isn't a car out there, no matter how good, in which the same effort couldn't be applied to something more important.

But the second is more encouraging, especially to those who, rightly, are engaged in campaigning against drink driving.

Relax. It's pretty much impossible anyway.

BROWN'S GREEN TAX – A BIT OF A GREY AREA

There are a few simple things I require of government ministers. Taking a broad view, I would be quite interested to know what they are going to do about the funding of the NHS, since it's a very complicated business and I won't pretend for a moment to understand it. A few of them have made it their lives' work, so I'm prepared to defer to them on that one.

On a more personal level, and since they are ultimately responsible for the people who might possibly be able to help me, I'd like to know what government is proposing to do about the bloke who climbed through my window and nicked my portable telly.

There are other issues that are no doubt their concern: the pensions crisis, benefit fraud, the war in Iraq, gay vicars (no, not gay vicars) and what the Monty Python team called the baggage retrieval system at Heathrow. These are all worthy of detailed study by suitably qualified people.

But what I don't need is politicians setting me an example, unless it's Charles Kennedy, since he likes a drink and so do I. I especially don't want them wasting valuable Commons time worrying about what sort of car I should drive, because I can work that one out for myself.

Apparently, some of these people are being offered the option of a ministerial Toyota Prius or a bio-fuelled Jaguar, while at the same time supporting a special tax on 4×4 cars in the interests of the environment. Nothing could be more irrelevant.

Let's assume, for the purposes of argument, that global warming is a real threat and that energy consumption is at the root of it. So that would make big, overweight and thirsty 4×4s a bad thing, obviously.

And what difference, exactly, is a tax going to make to that? If you're rich enough to run a big 4×4, a bit of extra tax isn't going to bother you. More to the point, how does tax save the planet? If 4×4s are such a bad thing, why doesn't the government simply ban them? I conclude that they don't want us to stop driving them at all. They just want some more money.

And the same goes for smoking. If lung disease is such an issue, and the government feels duty bound to do something about it, why isn't smoking illegal? Taking heroin is illegal, after all. The answer must surely be that smoking is ultimately good for the nation's coffers, and that nobody really wants us to stop. Same goes for binge drinking and driving around in cars.

I was asked to take part in a radio debate about this 4×4 tax business, and I dearly wish I'd been available to do so. On the panel was a man from an organisation called something like the Federation Against All-Wheel Drive; that's not quite right but I'm buggered if I'm going to dignify their mealy-mouthed cause by looking it up and getting it right. What I would say to this man is this: if you want to do something good for the world, can't you think of something better than preaching to us about the exact technical specification of the cars we're driving? Can't you go and make some soup for the poor, or mend some old dear's central heating boiler?

I'm not here to defend the motor industry, since it's big and ugly enough to do that for itself. But I will say this. In the 10 years or so that I have been writing about cars, it has made an unparalleled effort to clean up its act. My car today is between 20 and 50 times less polluting than the ones I struggled to own as a student. It caused less pollution during its manufacture, it causes less pollution in use, and it will cause less when it's thrown away.

What other industry or area of commerce has made a similar effort? Fashion? Construction? Other modes of transport? Publishing? Consumer electronics? I can't name one. Every now and then someone comes up with a totally fatuous statistic that shows, for example, how much less CO_2 would be produced if we turned our stereos off instead of leaving them on standby. Is that it?

Well, you might be thinking, the car was always a big culprit. But I'm not so sure. Figures I've heard state that road transport (and remember – that includes stinky Latvian tour buses as well as your Vectra) accounts for anything between 11 and 20 per cent of all so-called greenhouse gases. Even if it's 20 per cent, I'm left wondering about where the other four-fifths are coming from, and yet I hear nothing – *nothing* – about this in any populist debate about the environment. All I hear is some sanctimonious cant about how if I buy a slightly smaller car everything will be all right.

If I were in power, and I thought taxation was the sovereign salve for all environmental ills, here are a few of the things that would suddenly start costing you a lot more: vegetables grown in Israel and flown to your supermarket, when the same ones are growing just as well in England; replacement kitchens, since the one you have undoubtedly works perfectly well; bottled water from France, since there's perfectly good stuff in the tap; plastic carrier bags, which aren't even made here but are produced in places like China, and even if we recycle them they're sent back to China to be made into more carrier bags and then transported here in ships that burn thousands of litres of heavy fuel oil every day; and so on. These are real-world concerns at least the equal of the Volvo XC-90's fuel consumption. Yet the only person I know who talks intelligently on these matters is, remarkably, a car enthusiast.

I'm not going to be lectured about my driving habits by people who probably haven't bothered to check their loft insulation in the last decade. I have, as it happens, and I've improved it. Leave us alone, and leave our cars alone as well.

Still no news on the stolen telly, by the way.

ANY COLOUR YOU LIKE AS LONG AS IT'S AVAILABLE FROM DULUX

I've got the builders in this week. It's quite a big job – two new bathrooms, decorating throughout, plus a few structural alterations. The whole lot will probably take a couple of months to complete and after one week I'm already over budget, because I hadn't factored in the cost of sugar.

I favour a sort of post-modernist school lavatory chic look for the bachelor household, so on the whole have gone for white stuff. White walls, for example, and white porcelain. Wall tiles look suitably municipal in white and I only ever buy pure white bog roll.

But then we come to the question of the stairs, which have gone uncarpeted for years, the money allotted for the job going to Moto Guzzi. But this time I have studiously binned the Guzzi brochure and immersed myself in the John Lewis website instead. I was going to cover the entire floor in seagrass or some other form of monastic rush matting, but then I had a thought.

How would it look, I wondered, if the stair treads were alternately orange and lemon? That way I could start from a lemon hallway and arrive, purged by the acetic, at an orange landing. John Lewis sell both orange and lemon carpet, so it must be possible.

And then I thought a bit harder about the bathroom floors. White is all very well, and suitably redolent of those hotels situated on roundabouts in which I seem to spend so much of my life these days, but would a riot of terrazzo look better? Curiously, there is a shop just up the road specialising in the stuff, and they do a particularly nice lime-green version. Perhaps we have arrived at that apocalyptic moment in time when the avocado bathroom suite has once again become acceptable, too.

But that's the great thing about renovating the home. As Walt Disney said of animation, you can portray anything that the mind can conceive. There is a massive industry devoted to humouring your bad judgement and several TV programmes inspired by the idea of amateur designers ruining perfectly good houses through the medium of power tools.

No such indulgence from the motor trade. Most new cars come with perhaps half-a-dozen choices of standard interior trim, all of them very, very boring.

Even Porsche are guilty of this. My Boxster was available with just five standard interior colours. The options list featured another five. I went for a special dark-brown leather at huge expense and then paid more to have some panels in the black they would have been in had I not said anything. Yet when I look at it – monument to good taste though it is – I can't help thinking that it still has a leather interior like every other Porsche. I've only meddled in the colour scheme.

Meanwhile Jeremy, who has roundly denounced the Porsche and has spent two years proclaiming that the Honda S2000 is the best roadster money can buy, has bought a Mercedes SLK. Seven standard interior colours were available and in order to break free from the tyranny of German taste he had to resort to the bespoke and very costly 'Designo' range of hues. He now has black seats with red inserts. It looks quite good (though not as good as my Porsche, obviously) but why is it such a big deal? Red and black are hardly the new magnolia. Cars in the '50s had red and black interiors.

I wouldn't mind, but down at my local DIY super-store literally thousands of shades of emulsion are available, and all of them can be produced for you in a few minutes by a youth who wasn't charismatic enough to become an estate agent. The tile shop offers so much choice that I could tile the whole of my road without using any one design twice. Modern manufac-turing methods should mean that the same freedom is available to people specifying the seats, floor mats and facia of a new car. But what do we get? Biscuit beige, black and elephant-arse grey. Why? You wouldn't have that at home.

I do get the impression that the motor industry thinks we all need its guidance on matters of interior design. But this is ludicrous. Next time you're in a showroom, have a look at the salesman's tie. Would you let this man choose your new kitchen?

I've ordered the orange and lemon carpet, by the way. And the terrazzo. And I know what some of you are thinking: you're thinking that all this would look revolting. And you may be right, but since it's my house it's my business.

And if you don't like it you don't have to come and stay here.

PORSCHE OUTPERFORMS DESKTOP PRINTER – SHOCK

I spent this morning swearing at my computer printer. I'm no technophobe, but we have here one of those consumer devices assembled with superglue, inside which there are apparently 'no user-serviceable parts', so the only tool left in the engineer manqué's box is his 99-piece precision profanity set.

Here's the problem: it doesn't work. So I took it to the local computer shop, slapped it on the counter and explained as much to a man who should have been born with just two fingers. 'Ha ha ha,' he exclaimed, knowingly. 'How long have we had this, then?'

I have had it for five years.

'Well, that's pretty old tech now,' he explained patiently. 'You really need to upgrade.' Now, at this point a lesser man than me might have forked out for the new Epson Stylus Multijet 4.0 Megapixies and gone home happy. But not me. I wanted it mended. 'It's not economical,' he declared.

I appreciate, as everyone keeps telling me, that printers are remarkably cheap these days, but we're still talking about over £100 and that buys a lot of American Hard Gums. Furthermore, how much would my life be advanced by a new printer? Not a jot. I'd be back where I started, trying to print out a simple letter in response to an enquiry from a Mr Graham about music and motoring.

And it gets worse. Because I've had the computer for eight years it seems there is no longer a printer compatible with its old operating system. That means that in order to run the new printer, I'd have to buy a new computer as well, and learn how to use it. That would probably also mean buying a new 'docking station' for my infernal digital diary thing and probably some new upgraded miniature speakers for the CD player as well.

That would be a bit like going to Kwik-Fit for some new tyres and being browbeaten into buying a whole new car. Before you know it I'd have spent something like £1,500 on computer kit, and where would I be? Still sitting in front of an over-specified typewriter, still trying to send a letter to Mr Graham.

Things wear out, but it's not as if the old printer has had a hard life. It's probably produced a dozen pages a week since I've had it. 'Think how many pages that is,' said the computer man, triumphantly. Clearly, neither of us could in the heat of the moment but I've since worked it out and it's around 3,200, or perhaps 48,000 lines of type. Now think how many times the engine in my 106,000-mile 911 has rotated. I've worked that out as well and I think it's something like 6×10^9. One revolution of the flat six is one cycle of operation, like one complete sweep of the printer head, and yet the Porsche STILL WORKS PERFECTLY.

People bemoan the supposed built-in obsolescence of the car, but a better exemplar can be found in the world of digital tech. Those who promised that this stuff would be 'future safe' were simply driving us further into the hideous clutches of PC World and cluttering our lives with redundant plug-in transformers. In fact, the car always *was* future safe. You could pick any one from the collection in the Beaulieu museum and use it today on today's roads. Even the

Stanley Steamer is yours for the driving, so long as you can find a Welshman to dig up a bit more coal for you.

It's undoubtedly true that before the war the motor industry sold you a car, then after the war it started selling you fashion. The difference, though, is that we had a choice. You could embrace the new-fangled Ford Cortina, with its exotic foreign name and *faux* American styling, or you could do what my dad did and stick with the Morris Eight. The car has been good to us. The computer industry has simply filled my attic with old boxes.

You may be pleased to know that I eventually prised the lid from the bubblejet device and set to it with the little screwdriver from my Hornby train set. A few hours later and – hey printo! It whirred back into life and now sits on the desk in open defiance of Bill Gates and his evil henchmen.

I was very pleased with myself. But I couldn't help thinking that none of this would have been necessary if it had been made by someone like Vauxhall.

(Mr Graham has since received one side of A4 with about a dozen lines on it.)

MEN, RISE UP AND EMBRACE THE WHEELBRACE

As I've said before, there are no real gender issues in motoring. I don't doubt that the tastes of men and women differ slightly, but in an age when women run merchant banks and more and more men have hand-bags, their requirements are pretty much the same.

I do not believe, for example, that there is a specifically woman's view on motoring. I know some women who are as enthusiastic about motors as I am, and for the same reasons. I also know men who don't have a car at all because they think them the work of Beelzebub. Obviously these so-called 'men' are traitors to their sex, but that's the way it is.

And so to Drivesafe, a new initiative aimed at women motorists and accompanied by the inevitable 'handy pack' of helpful hints. Its authors point out that women do more town miles than men, and are therefore more at risk from threats such as road rage and car-jacking. Many of them, it is believed, lack the self-assurance needed to change a wheel. Drivesafe will show them how.

And on the face of it, that's a good thing. Men go shopping for clothes in the modern world, so it follows that women should be able to change wheels. What bothers me, however, is the suggestion that there won't be men on hand to do it for them.

If a woman suffers a puncture somewhere around town, then surely there will be a man somewhere – in another car, walking along the pavement, looking out of a window – who will put the spare on for her; a man who, denied by social development the opportunity to wear a lady's embroidered favour around his wrist as he rides into a jousting tournament against ye black knight on ye black horse, will relish the opportunity to wield the latter-day Excalibur that is the wheelbrace.

It seems not.

Cry sexist if you must, but this sort of thing really worries me. I'm not suggesting for a moment that a woman *shouldn't* be able to change a wheel, any more than I think some of my male friends should stop mincing around in the kitchen with tiger prawns and put some bloody shelves up. It's just that today's Guinevere of the road should be able to rely on Gawain in her moment of peril.

In any case, my quarrel is actually with the chaps. In the past few weeks I've watched three men attempt to change a wheel, and they all made a complete Horlicks of it. Cars fell off jacks, nuts were cross-threaded, and everyone had a good laugh. This is deeply symptomatic of a hideous blight affecting the modern British male; namely, that being a bit useless is perceived as being somehow endearing and 'blokeish'. Nothing could be further from the truth.

I keep meeting men who say things like 'Ha ha ha, I can't even wire a plug!' Why not? The instructions are usually moulded into the plug itself, or on a piece of paper pushed over the pins. If you can't wire a plug it's not because you are creative or because you have a left-hemisphere brain or because you're a bit of a bloke. It's because you are an imbecile.

Another man I met recently had employed a builder to screw a wine rack to the wall. Why he wants a wine rack anyway is a bit of a mystery, since he lives only a few doors from a pub that sells proper beer. Even more unfathomable is how he could bear the shame of standing by while another man drilled four holes in some brickwork and inserted some rawlplugs. He can regard himself as little more than a receptacle for keeping sperm at the right temperature until it's needed.

British men are facing a crisis. There are no world wars to fight, very little coal to be dug, no massive programme of railway expansion to feed. The forge is cold and the instruments of duelling are rusting above the fireplace in a country house experience somewhere. Poetry is unfashionable, as is serenading. Ballad-writers are noticeably thin on the ground. The attributes that once defined manliness are receding fast, already at such a low ebb that we can't even be relied upon to sort out a puncture for a distressed damsel. The roads are the last arena in which chivalry can be upheld.

I therefore wholly commend the Drivesafe initiative and in particular the handy pack that comes with it. I haven't seen it yet, but it sounds as if it's full of really useful advice on, among other things, changing wheels on cars.

I therefore think it should be distributed to all males over the age of 12.

HOW THE PEACE AND QUIET OF ENGLAND WAS RUINED BY THE NOISE OF PEOPLE COMPLAINING

As some of you may know, I've spent the last year learning to fly a light aircraft. Very satisfying it is too. It's something I dreamed about as a boy, ever since I picked up my first Air Ace Picture Library comic book and learned to draw something approximating to a Spitfire in the back of my maths exercise book.

But small aeroplanes aren't to everyone's liking. Richard Hammond, for example, whose crashing impatience renders him unable to appreciate the value of pre-flight safety checks, and who is not man enough to thank me when the wings haven't fallen off at the end of a journey.

And then there are the residents of the villages around my flying club's airfield, White Waltham in Berkshire. Some of them hate small aeroplanes because, apparently, they're noisy.

A bit of explanation is required here. A typical small airfield will have several runways – White Waltham has three – pointing in different directions to allow for changes in the wind. Each runway forms one leg of an aerial rectangle, around which the aeroplanes fly while preparing to land. These are called 'circuits', and those of us new to aviation spend a lot of time flying around them practising landings and take-offs. Given that each runway can be used in two directions, there are six circuits in operation at my airfield.

And the circuits are carefully designed to avoid overflying of the local villages, so that the residents won't be annoyed. However, there are a lot of villages and you don't have to stray very far outside the circuit before some old trout rings up the ops room with a complaint. This has happened to me.

People have rung up and, in effect, said, 'James May is flying his noisy little aeroplane over my garden, when he should be to the west a bit.' Well, what did they expect with my sense of direction? They should be grateful I haven't flown straight through the sitting room window or into the local orphanage.

But here's what really gets my goat. The airfield has been there since the '30s, when it was part of the vital Air Transport Auxiliary unit – the organisation that ferried newly built and repaired military aircraft to their operational bases. A lot of the ferry pilots were women, and you may have seen the famous picture, taken at the airfield, of a ripping brunette gal in flying kit standing under the nose of a gigantic Short Stirling. It's almost pornography.

So anyone who can remember when it was all trees would be over 90 and therefore deaf anyway. I doubt there are many people in the surrounding villages who bought their houses before the airfield was built.

In which case, people must have moved in knowing that there would be small aeroplanes flying around. But still they complain about it. This is like buying a house on a Barratt estate and complaining that there are people living next door. It's like me complaining about the sound of bells from the church down the end of my road. The church has been there for several hundred years, and it's not as if I wouldn't have noticed it when I viewed the house. There's a bloody great bell tower sticking out of it.

But no matter – I could probably complain to the authorities and someone would be obliged to look into it, when really Britain would be better served by someone coming around to tell me to stop whining and be grateful that the bells are there, ready to be rung when the EU invades.

Road noise? Well, everyone I know lives on a road of some sort, and they all either own a car or use taxis. A certain amount of noise is therefore to be expected. I would agree wholeheartedly that cars and bikes with wantonly loud exhaust pipes are an unnecessary evil, but that general thrum of traffic is just part of the sonic backdrop of modern life, like Radio 2.

And so, finally, to the *Top Gear* studio, which is based – da daah! – on an old airfield. It's the one where they used to build and test the Hawker Harrier, which you may know as a particularly noisy aeroplane. Those days are gone, and you'd think the locals would be glad, but you'd think wrongly. Some of them are now complaining that *Top Gear* is making too much noise.

Really? We're there, on average, about once a week. The airfield is very large, and we occupy the bit right in the middle with our test track. The nearest house is a long way away. I can accept that the steady drone of Clarkson shouting 'poweeeer!' would be quite irksome if you were relaxing in the garden of an afternoon, but the occasional and distant squeal of tyres around the Hammerhead is surely no more intrusive than the chirp of a randy blackbird.

But we live in an era when a single complaint has the weight of a 20,000,000-signature petition delivered to Downing Street. Consider the programme itself. If one person rings or writes to complain that Jeremy has been rude about the Liberal Democrats or that I've said 'cock', the producer is obliged to investigate it and do something about it. Why? Important work is being done at *Top Gear*. It's thanks to *Top Gear* that the new Koenigsegg has a rear wing, and that the motor industry knows not to waste its time and money trying to develop a convertible people carrier. If people had complained about Barnes Wallis's bomb bouncing through their back yards, or the *Flying Scotsman* making an irritating whistling noise, nothing would ever have been achieved and Britain would be renowned the world over only for being very quiet.

It's the same story with the flying club. The people who complain about the aeroplane noise forget that the person flying the airliner that takes them on holiday to Spain will most likely have started flying at a local airfield, often at great personal expense. If people like me weren't there supporting it by flying a wonky circuit over the village, everyone would have to go to Whitby on the train instead.

What else do these people complain about? Talking in restaurants? Babies crying at feeding time? Long grass rustling in the wind? Velcro? They could make a bigger contribution to the fight against noise pollution if they all simultaneously piped down.

Everybody shut up. You're beginning to get on my nerves.

IN CASE YOU'RE READING THIS ON THE BOG, HERE ARE SOME EQUATIONS OF MOTION

Professor Stephen Hawking once averred that for every mathematical equation he included in his book *A Brief History of Time*, the readership would be halved. This gives us:

$$Ra = \frac{Rp}{2^N}$$

(Where Ra is the actual readership, Rp is the potential readership, and N is the number of mathematical quotations. And if you think I'm making this up, it's all been checked by Yan-Chee Yu of the Oxford University Mathematical Institute. So there.)

This leads every other one of us rather neatly to the work of the Swiss scientist Daniel Bernoulli (1700–82), whose work on fluid flow showed us, in simplified form at least, that:

$$P + \tfrac{1}{2}\rho V^2 = CONSTANT$$

(Where P is the static pressure, ρ is the density, and V is the velocity.)

What Bernoulli was saying, in essence, is that when the pressure in a fluid system is reduced (by a constriction, for example), the velocity must increase, and vice versa. The rate at which the fluid flows will remain the same. It's hugely useful stuff if you design the air intakes for racing cars.

If, however, you are simply annoyed at being stuck in traffic jams at roadworks, you may prefer Bernoulli in its layman's form, which is known as May's

Motorway and Dual Carriageway Jam Avoidance Velocity Modulation Principle. This states that when one or more lanes of a busy multi-lane road are closed, the speed limit in the remaining lanes must be *increased* if the traffic is to keep flowing smoothly.

But here we arrive at a socio-political problem. For years it has been accepted that the most dangerous job in Britain is that of trawlerman. Recent research shows that a trawlerman is some 50 times more likely to be killed or injured at work than, say, me. If he is not despatched by the cold, the cruel sea or a rusty chain, he will be starved to death by the iniquities of EU fishing regulations.

A few years back he was briefly usurped by elephant handlers, since they are few in number but two had been trampled in quick succession, making the profession statistically unsurvivable. Roofers and glaziers are at considerable risk and aircraft carrier flight-deck crew should ensure that their children are well provided for. And surely no working man is in greater peril than the fitted-kitchen salesman who arrived uninvited at my door a few weeks ago just as I had finished reassembling (following a thorough clean) my Beretta.

But here are British road workers, suddenly at number 16 in the hit parade of hazardous jobs. In the last few years the number of deaths and serious injuries sustained by these people has risen sharply, from only one fatality in 2004 to four in the first half of 2005 alone. The Highways Agency is pretty sore about it, which is why motorways and dual carriageways are now strangled by sudden 30mph limits and all that 'lane closed to protect workforce' malarkey.

Quite right, too. No civilised society could possibly want to see its road workers in hospital. We'd quite like to see them mending the roads. By now you're thinking *what workforce?* and you may have a point. Over the last few weeks I have been monitoring these roadworks, and I have driven just over 26 miles at temporary speed limits past lanes closed supposedly to protect the workforce but without seeing so much as an endangered wheelbarrow. It would appear to be more a case of workforce staying at home to protect workforce. But I don't blame them. It's bloody dangerous.

So here is the solution. Roadwork should only be practised at night, when the traffic flow is light. Slowing to a constant 30 or 40mph for a few miles is really neither here nor there as far as total journey times are concerned. You can even calculate the difference it makes yourself:

$$T = 0{\cdot}857 \times D\left(\frac{60}{5} \times D \right)$$

(Where T is the extra time taken, D is the length of the roadworks in miles and S is the temporary speed limit.)

During the day, when the traffic is very dense, the workforce should stay away, since the traffic has to keep moving fast to prevent a total jam. At the same time, we can't really expect them to put all those bollards away every morning and so, in accordance with May's principle, the cars should actually speed up through the roadworks. For example, if only one lane is still open on a busy three-lane motorway, the speed limit should be 210mph. Or:

$$S = \frac{E \times L}{O}$$

(Where S is the new temporary speed limit, E is the existing speed limit, L is the number of lanes normally available and O is the number of lanes still open.)

I'd be amazed if anyone is still reading this.

IT'S A CAR, JIMMY, BUT NOT AS WE KNOW IT

It must be 20 years since Jimmy Savile told us that this is the age of the train, but maybe, finally, it is. Just as the last of the InterCity 125s he trumpeted so memorably terminates in the long rusty siding at the side of a scrapyard somewhere, things are looking pretty good on the permanent way.

I've been on three trains in the last month. Two between London and Manchester operated by Virgin Trains, and one from there to Hull operated by Northern Rail or something like that. I must admit that I preferred the era when one simply turned up at 'the station' and got on 'the train' instead of arriving at a retail and dining complex with some rails attached and then standing for an hour in front of a massive flickering monitor trying to work out which of a countless number of operators will accept the brightly coloured £135 stub in your hand. But still.

Apart from that, the whole experience was rather good. These were the new Pendolino trains; sleek, stylish and very cool. I know some railway commentators have criticised them for their weight and thirst, but they strike me as a Lexus amongst rolling stock. They are quiet, draught-free, smooth riding and very fast in an unflustered sort of way. The seats are very good, the upholstery subdued, the announcements intelligible. It's some years since I've been on a proper train and I was very pleasantly surprised.

For example, I'd reserved a seat. In the olden days this would mean there was a bit of cardboard wedged under the antimacassar, or was until some pissed pikey removed it, chucked it on the floor and then filled the table with empty Carlsberg cans so you felt better off in the concertina bit between the coaches.

Not any more. A little dot-matrix display above my place read 'Reserved, Mr May' so there was no argument about that.

There was still a chance that a zealous vicar or malodorous railway enthusiast would sit next to me but, again, I was lucky. For two of the journeys I had two seats to myself, and on the third I was joined by a woman who not only smelled rather nice but didn't speak to me at all, which was marvellous.

Crikey, even the buffet has improved. Once there was a slimy carriage offering the following range of sandwich fillings: cheese. Now there is a trolley piled high with fruit cake and pies and a big samovar thing for making hot drinks, a sort of wheeled five-star-hotel tea-and-coffee-making-facilities facility. Any more wine at all with your meal for yourself, sir? Why, yes.

What a pleasant and, as widely claimed, efficient way to travel up the sceptered isle. London to Manchester takes just two and a quarter hours, during which one may of course work on a laptop, read important documents or hold an impromptu meeting with colleagues. Obviously I did none of these things. I looked out of the window for a bit and then fell asleep with my head resting on the seat in front, dribbling on my trousers. But if you did work in IT or a customer relations role, you could annoy everyone else on the train by talking in a loud voice about managing expectations or tapping noisily on your strawberry personal organiser. You can't do that in the car.

However.

I said London to Manchester takes two and a half hours. Unfortunately, it's a place in London where I don't live to a place in Manchester where I don't want to be. And here we arrive at the crux of the public transport conundrum.

Obviously, long-distance communal travel makes sense. You wouldn't fly yourself to America in your own Cessna – you'd get on a big aeroplane with lots of other people and complete the bulk of the journey very rapidly. You wouldn't sail your own dinghy across the North Sea to Norway. You'd get on a ferry and stand around a bar with a load of lorry drivers and pimps. Lots of people seem to want to go from London to Manchester at any time, so they can all go together.

It's the little bits at either end of the journey that cause a problem, yet it's in the towns and cities that public transport is presented as the solution to all our woes. It's rubbish. If I'd had to find my way from Manchester Station to whichever hotel I was staying in using the local buses, I'd have given up and gone home again.

You can bang on all you like about trams, light rail, bendy buses and maglev, but until such things stop outside my front door in the space where I keep my car, they're not really any good. My local underground station – and the estate agent told me I was buying a property ideally situated for local transport facilities – is still 10 minutes' walk away, and with a big suitcase it's just too much trouble. No matter how comprehensive the public transport network becomes, there's always going to be a little bit of the journey requiring something personal.

And let's be honest here. Posh InterCity trains are generally full of respectable people, but local public transport isn't. I'm sure London tube commuters are largely upstanding pillars of society, but there are still enough of them that smell of old pants to make the journey unsavoury.

I have the solution. In my vision I step outside to find something like a Fiat Panda or Smart Car that doesn't belong to me but is open and starts with a simple button. There are no keys. I drive it to the station and leave it. Someone coming from Manchester then uses it to get to the offices around the corner from my house. Then someone else uses it to go to the shops. Occasionally they might pile up in one place or another, but in that case the people who we currently employ as traffic wardens are used to redistribute them a bit. It can't be any harder than running a bus service.

And you can't nick them, because they are electronically tagged to prevent them straying beyond a radius of a few miles. This is a simple matter, one of utilising the technology so readily used to punish us as a means of liberating us instead.

I can't really see why it wouldn't work. This is the age of the true city car – a car owned by the city.

PART 2 – THE FUZZY EDGE OF AUTOMOTIVE UNDERSTANDING

CHARLES DARWIN MAY BE ON TO SOMETHING

I'm always slightly surprised that my cat, Fusker, can't speak. I spend many hours talking to him, but it's always a totally one-sided conversation and the chances are that the only word he vaguely understands is 'Fusker'. And he can't even say that.

My other dependant, Woman, reckons he can't talk because he's only a cat, and that the evolution of cat technology is such that he just isn't capable of speech and for complex zoological reasons. But I'm not so sure.

In terms of the mechanics of speaking, the cat is as well equipped as I am. He has a voice box of sorts: a mouth, a tongue, teeth. These are what we use to form words. And yet still nothing of any consequence comes out of his witless furry face. Why?

I have been forced to conclude that Fusker remains speechless not because he is incapable of it, but because he has nothing to say. He has nothing to say because he hasn't done anything worth talking about. All he aspires to is another bowl of Munchies or the chance to go outside and look for a lady cat (even though he has no nuts, although he's too thick to realise this). He can communicate either of these desires with a simple bleat.

I suppose it's possible that some distant ancestor of Fusker, while chomping away at his cat food, came up with the design for a separate-condenser steam engine long before James Watt did. However, he could do nothing about it, so the idea went unrecorded. He could do nothing about it because he didn't have opposed thumbs, the very attribute that allowed humankind to fashion a pointy piece of flint into a farming tool and shake off the shackle of being a hunter/gatherer. It was a relatively small step from there to variable valve timing.

Since we're on the subject of tools I'd now like to talk about Mr Stanley and his famous knife. Any man who has owned a Stanley knife – and any man who hasn't is unworthy of his sex – will, at some point during the trimming of some linoleum or the assembly of a 1/72nd-scale Messerschmitt 109, have stuck the eponymous craft instrument into his body somewhere. This week, I drove mine into the fleshy end of the thumb of my left hand.

To all intents and purposes, I now have only one arm.

If you'd like to go and stick your own Stanley knife into your own thumb, you will discover how difficult many straightforward life skills can become. Grating cheese, for example, or playing Scott Joplin's 'Maple Leaf Rag' upon the piano. This is what separates us from the beasts of the field and hearth.

Consider driving. I hadn't realised, until it was clad in a *Beano*-style comedy bandage, just how crucial a role my left thumb plays in this everyday activity. Denied the use of this vital receptor, driving becomes notably more difficult. Even in my old Bentley, which, as a slovenly automatic, does more than pretty much any other car to relieve its owner of the tiresome duty of operating it, I find my finer points of car control slightly compromised.

All of which brings me, eventually, to modern car technology and driver aids, most of which have their basis in micro-electronics. They are amazing things. The injection system of a modern diesel engine can provide five separate squirts of fuel, each minutely timed and of minutely different volume, in the space of one ignition stroke – an event which, at 4,000rpm, occupies just under 0.004 seconds by my calculations. I couldn't do that.

A drive-by-wire throttle, when you depress it in anger at the exit of a corner, will garner information from sensors monitoring, among other things, air density and temperature, limits of traction and perhaps even the steering angle. At the same time, a disposable plug-in module will be deciphering the ignition requirements in three dimensions. I couldn't begin to sort this lot out even given three hours in a silent examination room with a calculator and my lucky pencil sharpener.

In fact, whatever computerised systems are responsible for these things are much, much better than me at punctuality, long division, data management and spatial logic. But I bet they couldn't catch a tennis ball.

I can. I can also ride a bicycle, swim, shoot clay pigeons and pat my head while rubbing my stomach. Bosch Motronic can't do any of these things. I could even, theoretically at least, compete in the triple-jump, and I bet I'd beat that robot Honda keeps banging on about.

So when people tell me that electronic controls are coming between the driver and the modern car, I say cobblers. Yes, the right-hand pedal in the new Golf GTi may seem a bit vicious at times, and perhaps the traction control in this or that supercar is too intrusive. I've no doubt that some electric power-steering systems are placing a barrier between the steering wheel and what the driving wheels are ultimately doing, and brake assist sometimes seems to make a mockery of the relationship between what we do with the middle pedal and what actually happens to the car. But to suggest that these things are usurping the driver is absolute nonsense.

Electronics are merely cussed and logical, as your desktop computer will ultimately prove to be. Meanwhile, the human computer is supreme, the most remarkable electro-mechanical device ever conceived and one as yet barely understood. I now realise that when I drive my old 911 down a winding country road, pretty much every last bit of my body save perhaps my hair is toiling away at the man/machine interface, deciphering the incomprehensible mass of information coming at it and translating it through the brain into a multitude of decisions and inputs. If you don't believe me, try it for yourself without one thumb, a big toe, an eye or a buttock. We are no closer to finding a substitute for the driver than we are to finding an alternative to sperm in the reproductive process.

The greatest driving aid in the history of motoring was fitted to the Benz Motorwagen when it was rolled out of its shed for the very first time, and it has been included in the design of every single car built since. It was you.

And it's still you.

NAKED MOTORCYCLE PORN SHOWING NOW

The late and still sadly missed LJK Setright had a rather pessimistic view of bike shows. He once described them as being 'full of people on crutches looking to buy their next accident'.

Personally, I rather like a good bike show. For a start, experience in my own garage proves that you can fit three or four bikes into the space occupied by one car, which means you don't have to walk as far as you do at the motor show. The fact that the biggest physical workout the average motoring journalist ever takes is three laps of the NEC while looking at cars strikes me as strangely ironic.

Secondly, the atmosphere is better at a bike show. Motorcycling is still largely a hobby, and has yet to be infected with much of the glitz and fatuous marketing cant that accompany the latest launch of a sporty lifestyle vehicle for the active-minded urban sophisticate. There's rather less carpet on the stands, rather more tepid lager in cracked plastic glasses.

And then there are the bikes. I admit that often, when I'm at home alone, I think I should give up motorcycling. I'm getting too old, too cautious, and I'm just not very good at it. I believe that 'waterproof motorcycle clothing' remains an oxymoron, and often, in the middle of a tight, greasy bend, I worry that Newton may have made a mistake, and there's some dark corner of physics where there is no equal and opposite reaction, and I'll fall off. But then I go to a bike show.

Nothing, and I mean nothing, tugs at the strings of my Neanderthal man-being quite like an array of new bikes, and especially the type of big-bore naked motorcycles that I like. It's something to do with the way engineering, styling and the dynamic considerations are required to collaborate in the design; their utter interdependence. A motorcycle really is an extension of your being on the road, and your own mass and dimensions are a critical aspect of the way the whole thing works. There is little room for conceit on the part of its maker, and it shows.

Because, on a naked bike especially, you can see it all. You can see the way the stylist and the mechanic have been forced to collude, to give and take, to work constructively together. Engineering considerations temper the excesses of artistry, artistry dignifies the metalworking. And it all chimes instantly with some need to climb aboard and imagine how the thing might feel, which is why bike shows are full of people sitting astride new machines and gazing blankly into the distance.

Take Yamaha's MT01 muscle bike. One side of the engine looks like the work of dour technologists with Rotring propelling pencils wedged into spring clips in their breast pockets; the other like the fantasies of some blokes in polo-necks who would be as happy doing fashionable kitchen appliances. It appears to have a fish poacher on that side; actually, I believe it's the cover for a filter. Marvellous.

This is why motorbikes make a better static statement than cars. Aston Martin boasts of 'power, beauty, soul', and the new V8 has it all. The power is in the superb engine, the beauty is in the sculpture of its bodywork, and the soul comes from the physical properties – the suspension set-up, the distribution of weight, all that impenetrable stuff – that make it drive the way it does. But on a motorshow stand we sense only the beauty, and feel only a distant longing inspired by some faint carnal promise. Meanwhile, the Ducati Monster is flashing its knickers at you like some metal harlot.

It was Dr Johnson, I believe, who said something to the effect that all men feel slightly inadequate who have not at some time been a soldier. Today, he might say that all men feel cheated who have not at some time owned a motorcycle. They have somehow resisted the silent siren cry it emits even when stationary; they have not succumbed to that visceral urge to crack open the throttle and feel the beast tremble, to quest alone and armoured like some latter-day knight of Arthur's circle.

It's there in all of us, which probably explains why bike-show exhibitors never really bother with the tiresome live-band and rollerblading displays that dog the car show. They know that there's still only one tune that really works for motorcycling, and that it will, whether we like it or not, be playing on a loop in the back of our minds, from the moment we arrive to the moment we leave with a bulging bag of brochures.

Stop fighting it. And get your motor running.

SOME OBSERVATIONS ON REAR-END HANDLING

We've had the Kyoto Summit, we've had the Good Friday Agreement, and we've had a United Nations resolution. And now I'd like all car manufacturers to sign an international gentlemen's agreement promising to leave my bottom alone.

I'm as liberal as the next man etc. etc. but this has now gone too far. What consenting individuals get up to in the privacy of their own homes is one thing; the dead hand of a multinational directed at my buttocks is something else altogether and, to my mind, wholly unacceptable. Is nothing sacred any more?

Now I think about it, I realise that the world's car makers have been showing an unhealthy interest in my plum duff for quite a long time. It started well over a decade ago with the widespread introduction of the heated seat, which for years has been hailed as a great thing on a cold morning. Even my 13-year-old Range Rover has seat heaters.

But here's a thing. It's been very cold for the few days prior to my writing this, and I've been doing quite a bit of driving. Yet at no point have I walked out of my front door into the frosts and hoars and thought, 'God in heaven, my arse is cold.' It never is. My buttocks are the second biggest muscles on my body and therefore retain a huge amount of warmth. I have cold toes, cold fingers, a cold nose, cold ears and cold hair, but none of these things are catered for in the cabin of the car. I suppose Mercedes has made some effort with that Scarftronic neck-warmer fitted to the new SLK, but otherwise it's hot cross buns as usual.

It didn't stop with the seat heater, of course. Some time in the mid-'90s I drove the first BMW 7-series fitted with the 'active seat'. The base of this 'stimulating innovation' could be set to gently rock your pelvis from side to side, supposedly in the interests of reducing backache and encouraging circulation. I tried it on a very long journey and it seemed to work, but I was very uncomfortable with the idea of a German technologist called something like Jurgen fondling my chuff at a distance.

Mercedes responded with that massage seat thing, which incorporates some fans to extract the *wurst* effects of the corporate lunch. But again, I have the feeling that Herr Doktor is taking an unhealthy interest in my tradesman's.

So far this has been a distinctly German thing, and I suppose it could be worse. It could be the British. Then the new Aston V8 would be fitted with a couple of spring-loaded horsewhips and you'd be scouring the cabin for a suitable piece of leather to bite on. Instead, it's the French who are now at it.

I've been driving the new Citroen C4 VTS, and I have to say there's quite a lot I like about it. It's a great-looking car, it has a sweet motor, it steers quickly and it's even reasonably quick. Obviously it's a bit sporty for my tastes but I imagine it would be ideal for the sort of people who regard trainers as shoes.

What I didn't like was the preponderance of buttons and knobs in the cabin. This sort of thing makes me nervous in a French car, since I've always believed the French to be poor at gadgetry and much better suited to pre-industrial activities such as cheese-making and erecting lavatories that don't flush.

You may remember, if you were watching *Top Gear*, that the C4 features a novel steering wheel on which the rim rotates but the middle remains stationary. As well it should, since I counted 17 buttons on it and even then I'm not sure I remembered to include the horn. If it went round and round as well you'd be in big trouble.

In fact I was so preoccupied with the steering wheel that I completely forgot about the C4's vibrating seat. Then I joined a motorway and the French got to work on my jacquesie.

This car is fitted with a device that senses the white lines of your motorway lane, and if you stray beyond them the seat performs a brief drum-roll on your bum. Not only that, but it's buttock-specific. Stray right and your right cheek gets a drubbing, stray left and so on. Unless you indicate, in which case the system reasons that you meant to change lane and leaves your derriere mercifully alone.

It sounds like a good idea, and in many ways it is. If you'd nodded off it would wake you up, certainly. For the lady motorist it may be a safer and more comfortable alternative to the vibrations that are apparently to be enjoyed on the pillion seat of any V-twin Italian motorcycle. Trouble is, I'm a chap and there are times when I don't actually need to signal to change lanes on a motorway, such as when I enter an empty contraflow in the middle of the night. Then it's a right pain in the butt.

I can't keep indicating for no obvious reason, or I'll end up looking like my mate Paul, who indicates even when he's turning out of a supermarket car-parking space. Or someone from the Institute of Advanced Motorists. Maybe you can turn the thing off using one of the buttons on the steering wheel, but at this point I was still trying to retune the radio.

I have to say I'm disappointed. I saw the genesis of this technology years ago on something called the Prometheus Project, a sort of non-competitive multi-manufacturer initiative to develop the driving aids of the future. This gave us sat-nav, intelligent cruise control, head-up displays, swivelling headlights and the lane-sensing system at the core of the Citroen's vibra-seat.

By my reckoning, all these things could be combined to allow me to join the motorway in London and then climb into the back for a kip until I arrive in Scotland. Instead, I've been given something to keep me awake. The motor industry has, as usual, aimed low, and humankind has been reduced to fiddling with each other's bottoms like the apes of the trees from which we have supposedly descended.

I think these people should stop arsing around and do something useful.

THE FUTURE OF IN-CAR ENTERTAINMENT

Some years ago I attended the launch of a new Daewoo MPV people-carrier type recreational vehicle, and realised immediately that I was at the dawn of a new era made dark by the lights of a perverted science.

Nothing to do with the Daewoo *per se*, since it was a perfectly conventional one-box family bus aimed at the sort of people who didn't see Marie Stopes for the true saint she was. At least, that's what I gleaned from the mutterings of my coevals. Couldn't say as much with any certainty myself, since I didn't actually drive it.

No – from the moment we arrived, it was quite clear that the new Daewoo was not aimed at the driving enthusiast, or indeed any sort of driver. It had been designed to keep your kids quiet on a journey, and to that end was equipped with video screens, DVD players, gaming consoles and individual headphone sockets, all of which were installed in the back. So that's where I spent the test drive, having recruited a journalist and photographer partnership from a rival publication to act as surrogate dad and dad up front.

And I hated it. I'm not a Luddite, but these X-boy things really do drive me up the wall, and if I were a parent I would worry that my children were going to grow up with hideously overdeveloped thumbs and atrophied fingers. I also can't quite see the pleasure in watching a film in the car, since it will almost certainly have been made in America and why would you want to look at that when England is just outside the window?

These days everyone is offering this stuff. You can have it as optional equipment on dozens of cars, and you can buy after-market sets that end up looking as though they were wired up by Italians. It's all very well, but I can't help thinking that this kind of thing will drive us further into the hideous embrace of the Dr Mengele of our times, i.e. Dixon's.

And so, as we creep inexorably towards what the AA always calls the Great British Bank Holiday Exodus, here are a few simple (and free) in-car games designed by me and my colleague Richard Hammond on long journeys. All are resolutely rooted in an era when we made our own entertainment.

That's your car (2 players)

Drive along normally. When you spot a really hideous car, either parked or in the next lane, shout, 'See that? That's your car!' before the other bloke does. At the end of the journey, the player with the worst car is the loser.

Take five (2 players)

The object of the game is to secure the best car from the next five that pass in the opposite direction on a quiet road. Selection cannot be revoked, and either player may go first. Player 1 may choose the first car to pass, in which case Player 2 must choose from the next four. There may be a better one, there may not. He has to have the fifth car if he has not chosen already. Player with the best car wins that round.

Longest finger in the world (any number)

This is ideal for Channel Tunnel crossings, ferries to the Isle of Wight or any other circumstance in which passengers are confined to a stationary car with a roof-mounted whip aerial. Remove the aerial and hand to player 1. Holding it by the threaded end, he must perform a pre-ordained facia task using the bendy opposite end, against the clock. Tasks can include retuning the radio or setting automatic climate control to a particular temperature and stratification. Fastest time wins. Note that the radio retuning on auto seek may be compromised by the missing aerial.

In-car air-vent virtual fountain (any number)

Another one for a stationary moment, or even for children in the back. Take an irrelevant page from the owner's handbook – say the one about the dangers of eating any part of the battery – and tear it into thin strips, three per player. Find a role of sticky tape. The object of the game is to secure your three strips to your personal air vent and adjust the airflow and angle such that the paper strips form a perfect Prince-Of-Wales feathers display. Best one wins.

Dashboard spot-the-difference (2 players)

Player 1 studies the dashboard and centre console for 15 seconds, noting the position of all knobs and switches and the reading on any displays. He then looks away while Player 2 alters one thing. On a given signal Player 1 then has another 15 seconds to spot the difference. Things that may be changed include settings for heater controls, the time, the radio display, the position of column stalks and so on. On old Range Rovers some knobs can be removed altogether. This may happen anyway.

My, how the long miles fly past!

THE TECHNICAL REVOLUTION IN THE TOYSHOP

You'd be forgiven for thinking that the motor industry is at the molten core of that white heat of technology thing we've heard so much about. But I'm not so sure.

A cursory investigation into the progress of the car reveals that it has actually been a pretty cautious and conservative affair. There have been a few highlights, such as the Mini and the Citroen DS, but none of the quantum leaps we've seen in aviation. And so much of what we considered new developments in the car – supercharging, turbocharging, fuel injection, variable valve-timing, anti-lock brakes, composite materials, sat-nav, fuel cells – were handed down from above.

Now it turns out that the situation is worse than I thought. I recently worked on a BBC programme about my favourite childhood toys, and it transpired that much of what the motor industry has touted as new ideas over the last decade could be revealed as old hat after a quick rummage around the attic.

Take the business of platform sharing. If this has ever confused you, I should explain that a car's 'platform' is essentially the floor of its bodyshell, plus perhaps a bulkhead or two. The platform is responsible for much of a car's structural integrity and crash-worthiness, and therefore its design consumes a dispro-portionate amount of the total engineering effort. Sharing them between several models makes obvious sense.

Students of fashion and advocates of greater choice will say this is a good thing, since it spawns a greater variety of cars. The Audi TT, for example, is essentially a Golf underneath, and would probably have died on the drawing board but for this simple manufacturing expediency. The outgoing Alfa Spider was based on the Fiat Tipo, and the previous generation Porsches Boxster and 911 were more closely related than you might think.

Meanwhile, connoisseurs of the car say it's a bad thing, because all these so-called 'niche models' are hamstrung by the dynamic attributes inherent in the common platform. Both groups have a point, but neither should imagine this is anything new.

If you have a Tri-ang *Flying Scotsman* kicking around the house (it was their best seller, so you may well do) you already own an exemplar of platform sharing; by which I mean the platform on which the engine is built, not the one at which it stands. At the advent of Tri-ang Railways in the early '50s, the model railway was already a very old idea, but model railways were either very crude or very expensive. Tri-ang's genius was in producing something convincing and accessible, and they did this by reducing the number of rolling stock 'platforms' they needed. With a relatively small handful of locomotive chassis, electric motors, coach bogies and wagon frames they produced the biggest range the world has seen. It was all affordable, too. Closer to home, Scalextric was up to something similar. And VW thinks it's been clever in using that Golf platform for a handful of Skodas.

'Modularity' is something else that the motor industry has been very smug about, especially in relation to engine designs in which one cylinder 'unit' can be multiplied to form a variety of configurations. But what is Lego if not unutterably modular? Architects love the stuff: it can be used like real bricks to build miniature houses, large bricks can be used to replicate the sub-assemblies of pre-fabs, and individual bricks can even represent whole buildings in models of entire towns. This stuff has been around since the '40s.

Interchangeability of parts? It sounds impressive but Meccano showed the way over 100 years ago. Indeed, its creator Frank Hornby (later of trains fame) was inspired by the apparent standardisation of components used in the day-to-day machinery of late Victorian Britain – cranes and so forth. Any two parts from any two Meccano sets in history are completely compatible, even the nuts and bolts. Will Mercedes-Benz be saying that in 2105?

Remember all that fuss about the Japanese technique of poke yoke? It's a system of foolproofing, of designing components such that they will only go together in the correct way. Build the Airfix 1/72nd-scale Heinkel 111 and you will understand it perfectly. The locating pins on the two engines are positioned in such a way that you simply cannot build them the wrong way around. That kit came out in 1962, by the way.

I said in my programme that the story of toys is the story of everything: of society, of the economy, and most importantly of new manufacturing techniques. Closing the lid on my virtual toybox and returning to my normal day job, I find myself somewhat disillusioned.

I think it's high time the car industry stopped playing around and gave us something really new.

THE BEST DRIVING SONG IN THE WORLD EVER

Of all the senses, smell has the greatest power to evoke. It is impossible to remember a smell and you cannot imagine a new one, so there are no smells in the future. That means a particular scent, such as a perfume that once wafted from the dove-like neck of a loved one, has the power to come crashing through our ordered lives like a lager lout at an elegant cocktail party.

Next to smell comes sound, particularly music and especially pop music. Even now, somebody, somewhere, engaged in something menial such as washing up, and with the radio on in the background, has been transfixed because the distant and obfuscated memory of some personal reckoning has just been thrown into crystal-clear relief by the Electric Light Orchestra's 'Mr Blue Sky'.

I mention all this because for the new series of *Top Gear* we've devised a survey to find the nation's favourite driving song. The people send in their suggestions, we whittle them down to a shortlist and then you vote for the overall winner. Usual sort of thing – we got the idea from some other programme about houses or famous inventors.

Since we intend to arrive, once and for all, at the best driving song of all time, this is worthy of some thought. We would urge you, for example, not simply to think of a song with 'car' in the title (e.g. 'Driving in My Car' by Madness), or to nominate the Sweet's 'Blockbuster' because it has a police siren at the beginning, or the Stones' 'Honky Tonk Women' because there's a car horn in it that still takes you by surprise. Essentially, the competition is open to any song, so something by Black-Eyed Peas is up there against the Elizabethan lute song 'Fair, If You Expect Admiring' by Thomas Campion.

But we all know that this is really about pop – old pop, which was at first ephemeral, being of a time and for that time, but later has the power to mug you simply because it has lain outside the sphere of your existence for so long, having been borne away and dispersed on the very ripple that made it meaningful.

To placate the pedants, I should say that by 'pop' I mean anything that might once have been played on Radio 1 or your local station, and which is now heard on Radio 2. The radio is where pop belongs.

Contrary to the beliefs of my *Top Gear* colleagues, my music collection does extend beyond 1750 and does include quite a bit of pop. Some of it is even on CD. Curiously, they have almost all been bought on or for car journeys, because your standards are different in the car: what you listen to, what you eat, whether or not you shove your finger up your nose. I would never listen to AC/DC's 'Let There Be Rock' at home, but the other day I bought it for the car, thinking it might usher in some forgotten moment from the memory of a memory that is my teenage years.

But of course, it didn't work, because I knew what was going to happen. It may have made me drive a bit more vigorously, but then, so does *The Archers*.

Compare this with an experience I once had in Detroit, driving around in the evening in a Cadillac I'd borrowed. The radio was tuned to the local pop station and chuntering away in the background, when suddenly I heard, and immediately turned up, Wang Chung's 'Dance Hall Days'. I had lived constantly with this song for a few months when I was 16, but then it had disappeared. Here it was again, completely unexpected, and the benign ghosts of my own dance hall days filled a car thousands of miles from home and over two decades removed from the original events. The effect was so electrifying that I turned on to an empty freeway and just cruised, not caring where I was, until it was over.

That night a DJ didn't save my life, but he did remaster a crackly old part of it so that I could enjoy it again.

That's why pop is best on the radio, and why pop on the radio is best in the car. The car is like a giant personal stereo, but one over which you should never have control. Instead, it's left to someone in a dark, stuffy booth somewhere to press the buttons that reprise snippets of your life that you would never have been able to recall so clearly without the right soundtrack.

Please vote in our greatest driving song survey. Just write your suggestion on a postcard and send it in, no explanation necessary. I'm thinking about it even now, and I have a feeling that my best driving song will be something I haven't heard for 20 years.

HOW TO DEAL WITH VAN DRIVERS

I'd like to do my bit to promote the spirit of goodwill this Christmas by proposing a new solution to the age-old problem of road rage.

I have to say that one part of me doesn't actually believe in road rage. Recently, I narrated a BBC series on this very subject, and it struck me that no one involved actually suffered from road rage at all. Judging by the testimonies of their wives, children and friends, they simply had rage. They raged at home as well, and probably in pubs and shops too. They were just angry people who were especially unhappy about having to work as a sales rep or drive a diesel.

On the other hand, there are some unbelievably rude bastards out there. I've met several of them recently; not people who drive carelessly, but people who are hellbent on starting a fight for no earthly reason. What to do? One school of thought – and one I would normally subscribe to – says you should smile, wave and drive on. Then again, this is running away, and though a perfectly acceptable tactic when you're nine and you've been caught scrumping apples, it's a bit spineless when you're a grown man with principles and some bloke has just tried to kill you with his van.

I suppose that in this age of justice, no-win-no-fee legal aid and the European Court of Human Rights, the civilised thing to do would be to assemble witnesses, take action and seek recompense through the law. But this would be messy, time-consuming and a burden on a legal system that has more important things to deal with. It would probably also involve some paperwork, which is the work of Satan.

No, the only way to sort this out – and provide an enjoyable spectacle for motorists stuck in traffic jams, to boot – is with a duel. I think society may have lost sight of the benefits of formalised combat as a means of solving petty disputes. Brawling is unacceptable. The law is tiresome, somehow inconclusive, and will leave seething resentment in its wake. Duelling is the answer.

But before you rush off to demand satisfaction from an aggressive van driver (you may have guessed by now that I have a bit of a beef with van drivers this week), there are a few things you should know. Duelling is now highly illegal, but as you will have despatched a van driver, no jury is likely to convict. Also, duelling should properly be conducted in accordance with a complex etiquette first laid down in the *code duello* of Renaissance Italy, but this is probably due for an automotive update.

The offended man should, strictly speaking, instigate proceedings with 'some inescapably insulting gesture' such as throwing a gauntlet before his opponent. Quite why this is such an affront I don't know, especially as most people would simply pick it up and say, 'Here, mate, you dropped one of your gloves.' Therefore I propose a new convention, such as holding up a card bearing the likeness of the late and much lamented former chairman of Aston Martin, Victor Gauntlet.

At the discretion of the wronged party, and for the full mother-he-has-killed-me-dies effect, the duel can be fought to the death. But it is acceptable to fight to 'first blood', in which case, once you have brought forth the crimson fluid from the van driver, he is deemed to be the loser. This is good enough, even if *you* lose, because whatever status you think might be accorded to phat alloys or a big stereo, it's a livid two-inch scar on the right cheek that gets the girl.

For the van driver to decline the duel is dishonourable and effectively means he's lost. That's about it, really, as far as swordsmanship on the central reservation is concerned.

So to the man in the Renault Trafic who tried to run me off my bike last week, I say to you, sir, that your beard is not well trimmed, and that I can offer you the services of a blade.

And to the man in the Sprinter who tried to ram me: sir, I put it to you, sir, that you are indeed driving like an arse, sir. And I shall run you through, sir.

And to the man in the flat-bed Transit, who asked what thou art to do about it, thou great poof: very well, look your last upon the sun.

How refreshing is this? Under the current conventions for dealing with road rage, we arrive at our destinations boiling with a suppressed fury that we then inflict upon those we love. But a duel is clean, dignified and honourable. A duel, once over, can be quickly forgotten.

Especially if you're dead.

(James May is currently smitten through the helm and, without help, cannot last till dawn.)

BE AFRAID. BE VERY AFRAID. BUT ONLY OF
THE SIZE OF THE BILL.

In the past, I have lamented the efforts of boring motor-related businesses to promote themselves with the findings of a fatuous survey or two.

Then I noticed that they'd changed tactics, and had started dispensing banal advice about winter driving or foreign motoring holidays in an attempt to make their industry seem more newsworthy than it really is.

But the latest efforts by Purple Parking to avoid paying for a proper advert actually defy belief. The company that is now branded purpleparking, its last remaining space having been sold off for £9.95 per 24-hour period or part thereof, is claiming that its London Heathrow car park is haunted. Spooky, really, because the last time I used the 50-acre site – where 'strange noises and sharp changes in temperature have been reported', and where during the day a car is parked every 20 seconds, it says here – I could have sworn that the LCD read-out on the ticket machine briefly displayed the image of Jacob Marley, who, as we all know, is as dead as a doornail.

Clearly, it's all complete rubbish.

I speak as someone who has indulged in a spot of genuine ghost-hunting. I once stayed, on successive nights, in three of the allegedly most haunted houses in England, Scotland and Wales, and I honestly wouldn't recommend the experience to my worst enemy. I left each one in great haste pursued by every demon that has ever dwelt within the minds of men. So I consider myself well qualified to comment on these matters.

And while I love a good fireside chiller as much as anyone, I'm afraid purpleparking's just doesn't stand up. 'When the airport has shut down for the night and we have said goodbye to our last customer, an eerie calm descends,' they say. This is not because the vacant spaces are stalked by unquiet souls who could have sworn they'd asked for a VAT receipt but now can't find it. It's because everyone has gone home.

Undeterred, however, paranormalparking's marketing boss Steve Waller has adopted the mantle of an opium-addled Victorian novelist. 'Looking for inspiration while working late in the office I have taken a walk around the compound and twice caught the fleeting impression of people talking,' he writes. 'But heard as if through a wall.' It may be a piece of undigested airline food etc. At least he resisted the urge to say it was a dark and stormy night.

Now PD James, she's one who could summon the dead hand of mortal dread with a story about a haunted dolls' house or whatever. And Dickens recognised that the lonely signalman, marooned in his box, deep in a damp cutting and with nought but a chipped tin mug and the fevered workings of his consumptive imagination for company, was simply asking for a visitation from the other world.

But car parks just aren't scary. The bloke in charge usually has a modern hut with a telly, a telephone, a radiator and tea- and coffee-making facilities. He's hardly a soul in torment, and if he has an idle moment he will probably watch a repeat of *Top Gear* rather than allow his mind to dwell on aspects of the occult.

Mind you, to be fair, if I found myself in purpleparking's lot late at night and I came upon the marketing director wandering around, wearing the chains he forged in life, and trying to dream up new promotional initiatives for what is, when all's said and done, just a car park, I might be slightly disturbed.

Late last night I rang purpleparking's office to see if there was Anybody There, and to ask if there was any substance to this story, or if it was just a desperate ploy to hoodwink unsuspecting motoring columnists in quality broadsheet newspapers. I was assured by a voice, rising as if from the tomb, that the unexplained events at their Southall operation were a very serious business.

Well, I'm sorry, but I just don't believe in PR. The simple fact is that the car and its related service industries have never, to my knowledge, yielded a decent ghost story. There have been phantom ships, ghost trains, aerial carriages hauled by demented skeletal horses. But a quick perusal of my gazetteer of British hauntings has revealed not a single apparitional Austin Seven with a headless driver pulling noiselessly into a business car park to the abject terror of its attendants.

The car park is too new, too temporal and just too mundane to invoke the spirit world, real or imagined. The worst you're likely to confront is the spectre of an expired credit card at the exit barrier.

I'M GAY, BUT NOT THAT GAY

This weekend, I've come out. Sorry to hit you with it so bluntly, but there really is no easy way to admit to being gay even in this era of rampant inclusiveness.

I realise, too, that no one really wants to read a lot of cloying self-analysis from someone who can't accept, in the post-Wilde era, that it's of no real interest to anyone. No – I mention it simply because there is an important message for the modern motorist within all this.

I also wish to make it absolutely bloody clear, right here in paragraph three, that I'm not really gay at all, and that I've simply been coerced by circumstance into a temporary gay lifestyle experience. On the other hand, I'm forced to admit that there's a lot to be said for it.

It all began on Friday afternoon when, with a tra-la-la, Woman departed the May household to spend a weekend in Italy with her posh mates. Nothing too debilitating about that. Not being one of these useless modern men, I can cook, clean, shop and make my own entertainment.

But then my mate Colin rang to say his wife had left him for the weekend as well. Regular readers may remember Colin is a bloke who never puts spanners back in their proper place in the toolbox. I invited him round and we immediately set to work stripping and rebuilding the back end of an old motorcycle.

Obviously, this quickly degenerated into a huge barney over the number of tools left lying on the floor, but because we're chaps it was all soon forgotten, with no hard feelings, so we went to the pub to play darts.

Then we had a huge curry, came home, cracked open a bottle of chilled Orvieto and settled down on the sofa together to watch *Where Eagles Dare*.

By the end of this we were in a bit of a state and it made sense for Colin to stay over. So I installed him in the spare room with a copy of *GQ* and went to bed.

The next day, over a gargantuan breakfast in the nearby café, we had to acknowledge that, bar the sleeping arrangements, we had become a bit gay. But since we were enjoying it, we thought we might as well carry on. The warm bosom of womanhood has much to recommend it, yet there is a unique bond between men that dare not speak its name but will compel them to go over the top together for sheer love of camaraderie. Also, and despite being a bit of a clean queen, I found I didn't really care what Colin had done to the towels in the downstairs bathroom.

And so, after watching the aerial combat scenes in *Battle of Britain* (while fast-forwarding through that tedious bit where Susannah York prances around in her pants), we went shopping.

We – I mean I – needed some new crockery and several other items for the home. Now I have always regarded any form of cohabitation as rather unnatural, and balked at those tiresome conventions of domesticity that manifest themselves in a mealy-mouthed desire for co-ordinated housewares. But in a famous department store I was struck by how much more pleasurable this sort of thing is as a couple, and by the realisation that greater love hath no man than this, that he lay down his spare time to help his special friend choose some poncy plates. Colin even bought me a pub lunch.

I realised, though, that our diet was sorely lacking in Omega B supplements and free radical scavengers. On the way home we diverted to a supermarket, where I bought the ingredients for dinner while Colin had a free-trade cappuccino in a nearby coffee bar, in case anybody saw us. That evening, after another round of killer on the *Cross Keys* oche, I cooked my partner free-range shepherd's pie with a medley of organic vegetables, washed down with a couple of bottles of a robust burgundy. By now we were beyond the point where the subject of staying over even had to be raised, and after watching *Cross of Iron* over a few large whiskies, we went to our separate beds.

The next morning, while Colin knocked up some crumpets, we decided we'd earned a proper day out. An air display in Wiltshire sounded promising. It was a fine day, we could take a picnic and a blanket and I could do the crossword lying in the sun (although Colin doesn't like this because he says it means I won't talk to him). We could also enjoy a pleasant drive in the country.

And here we arrived at the acid test of our relationship; the equivalent, in a normal heterosexual coupling, of that first audible fart. Could we, as two grown men now totally comfortable in each other's company, drive through London in my Boxster with the roof down?

No.

THE BUILDING BLOCKS OF THE CAR OF THE FUTURE

As a schoolboy, I found car design rather frustrating. Long before the days of the laptop and laser printer, all we had was the squared paper in the back of a maths exercise book and the coveted Oxford Mathematical Instruments Set in its burnished metal tin.

The hours we spent on this sort of thing! You knew that car design had taken an unhealthy precedent over algebra when the two met somewhere forward of the staples in the middle of the book, which was always difficult to explain when you were sent to the stock room for a new one.

But there was something about the design language of the mid-'70s, the tyranny of graph paper and the obvious limitations of a plastic set-square, that led the artless youth inevitably to a Volvo 244 or the early Lotus Esprit. Pages of them.

Later, there was real engineering drawing, with a much greater range of drawing tools and much bigger pieces of paper. Yet it was still pretty difficult once you deviated from the rectilinear and attempted anything as curvaceous as a car. And because it was something of a matter of kudos to have the hardest pencil in the school – I had an 8H – most of my designs ended up in slices.

Back at home, there was always Lego. Lego was great for aeroplanes, with the eighter and fourer blocks being staggered to give the semblance of a fuselage and the flat plates forming wings. It was also good for waterline models of supertankers: the superstructure of these things is essentially blocky.

Still, not much cop for cars, though, and the problem is one of resolution. A boy's small box of Lego bricks is to car design what Teletext is to cartography (see the weather pages). To render a convincing curve, or even the suggestion of one, you need to make an enormous model out of thousands of blocks; with just a few dozen even the Lotus is impossible. It's why digital cameras have millions of pixies in them. It's also why the Lego Pudsey Bear at the BBC *Children in Need* office is about four feet high. The reason his face and ears have been slightly remodelled is because I became bored and consequently drunk at a BBC party.

But now I have discovered – and about 30 years late, as with most things in my life – Lego Technic. It's not really like normal Lego at all; more a sophisticated plastic Meccano, with myriad connectors, beams, shafts, gears, motors, wheels, springs and so on. It all clips together, avoiding the misery of sore fingers from endless nut-and-bolt work.

On my desk I have my completed Lego Technic Ferrari, all 18.5 inches and 719 components of it. The box declares that it is suitable for anyone over the age of eight, which I am.

The beauty of it is this: where normal Lego failed to allow me complete self-expression where the shape of cars was concerned, Lego Technic allows me complete liberty to build the guts of them. This is much more interesting, in my opinion, since styling is essentially about fashion, but the stuff inside is engineering. Spaceframes or chassis can be made in almost infinite variety. There are wishbones and suspension parts, stub axles and a steering rack. There is a V10 engine whose tiny crankshaft and pistons can be viewed moving through transparent cylinders, and as these cylinder units are genuinely modular and the crank is a built-up item, the motor can be rebuilt in other configurations.

There is even a differential: not a representation of one, but a miniature working version of the real thing that must be assembled. It's brilliant and genuinely educational, since a differential is impossible to explain to, and even harder to draw for, anyone who asks how one works. Here it is, in plastic. I've heard amateur child psychologists and enthusiasts of 'creative play' claim that all this is too much for young people, but I disagree. Children are brilliant at this sort of thing. It's why Victorian Britain prospered – we put them in factories.

Being spiritually not much more than eight, I've started dismantling the Ferrari in the belief that I can improve it. Being in reality more like 43 and with fading eyesight, I probably can't. But maybe somebody with a satchel somewhere can.

We know that the engineers Moulton and Issigonis tinkered endlessly with Meccano in designing a certain revolutionary small car. Lego Technic is not ultimately quite as versatile as Frank Hornby's famous constructional toy, but it's not far off and much more finger-friendly than the old metal stuff.

And that's why you should buy Lego Technic for your kids. Somewhere in this pile of plastic parts is the next Mini.

THIS IS PERSONAL

Sally-Ann Naylor, assuming that's your real name, you look like a nice gal, with your summery floral skirt and your big cuddly jummy with the floppy collar, and that explosive smile with the perfect teeth at its epicentre. I like you already.

But have you really paid £499 for the number plate SN05 SAN, just because it features your initials? Who's going to know? You'd have to be buying £500-worth of ammunition for a known gun psychopath before that looked like a sensible purchase. You S1 LLY B1 TCH.

And look, Robbie Paul Arnott: you might otherwise be a good bloke to take to the pub. I admire your flagrant disregard for the conventions of smart dress and your comedy haircut. But since you've spent £499 on RA05 RPA, I've decided that you're a bit of a SAD 61T.

Elsewhere, I've seen an advert from the DVLA showing a man in a mud-caked stripey shirt clutching the registration plate RU04 GBY. I hope people pull up next to him at traffic lights and say, 'Hey, I bet you play ruohfourgby.' Daft BUG 63R.

Thanks to the selfless efforts of my ancestors, I am not a number. I am a free man. Yet these days it seems you're nobody unless you're someone on your number plate. If only my parents had been blessed with the foresight to have me christened JAM 3S.

Getting hold of a personalised registration number used to be a complicated and expensive business. If I remember it rightly, you had to acquire the remains, or at least the identity, of the complete car bearing the number you wanted. For this reason a lonely crofter living in the wilderness with his Austin Seven reg JM 1 would one day find himself accosted by some terrifying captain of industry in a Rolls-Royce offering him £20,000 for his car. So the old system had a sort of self-regulating mechanism built into it; it cost big money and it had to be something really good to warrant the trouble and expense.

But the whole number-plate business has been liberated, with the inevitable result that some purveyors of 'distinctive marks' are taking the P155 NOW. I note that 2 XX is up for sale at a staggering £29,950. Unless both your names are Xavier, why would you want this? What does it say about you, other than that you have more MON 3Y than S3 NSE? And why would you want the registration number A740 BMW? If you own a BMW 740, it will already say as much on the bootlid.

Every T110 MAS, D1 CKS or HAR 13Y wants a personalised registration plate these days, and with catastrophic results. Some of the offerings currently advertised in my pile of car mags are just plain cringeworthy. Does R19 MEO look like 'romeo' to you? It does? May I suggest you stop driving immediately. Does J4 DFS really say 'Jade's'? MYA 35E it does. Do you expect people to be impressed? I'm going to think you simply can't SPE 1L.

Look, Mr P Gent: paying several thousand pounds for P9 ENT is a grave M15 TAK, because a 9 does not look like a G even through the wrong bit of your bifocals. And if you happen to be called Barry, I would counsel against buying 134 RRY because that's not your name. It's not even a word. And when people find out you spent £9,995 on it they're going to think that YOU 51R are a bit of a TOS 53R.

Viz comic once famously pointed out that it was much cheaper to change your name to match the number plate you already had than fork out for a personalised one. I've come up with another idea. I'm going to claim that the letters in my registrations are actually clever acronyms. Thus the Bentley's, TOY 102W, means 'Tiller Of Yacht' and the SPF 856R on the Jag advises of a 'Suspicious Puddle in Footwell'.

On second thoughts, this is a RUB 15H idea. I've also noticed that the Bentley's number looks like it could be meant as a personalised one, so I'll have to write to Classic Nouveau Registrations and request something completely meaningless instead. This is going to be a tough call for an organisation that thinks SA02 RAH says 'Sarah'.

There is no more tragic testimony to our society's self-obsession than the personalised number plate. If you really think I need to know that your name's Terry, just get a big felt tip and write 'T3rry' on the rear bumper. Unless you're the stationery magnate I once met who had the registration number A4 PAD, no one is going to be impressed.

Please, please stop it. It's not B1 GOR C13 VER.

IS IT A CAR? IS IT A BIKE? NO. AND NO.

Attempts to combine the virtues of the car and the motorcycle in a single machine have rarely been successful. An early example was the so-called motorcycle combination, a German development. Originally, this comprised a normal motorcycle fitted with a wheeled platform on to which a Spandau machine gun was mounted. However, its makers soon discovered that it was impossible to ride the bike and work the gun at the same time.

Rudimentary bodywork was added to the gun platform and a second German installed with the sole job of firing the weapon, leaving the original rider free to operate the motorcycle's controls and shout 'Himmel!' when a wire, stretched across the road by the French Resistance, sliced his head off. Unwittingly, the sidecar had been born.

After the war, British bike designers refined the idea, removing the machine gun, installing the wife, and thus creating a means by which the motorcycle licence holder could transport the nuclear family, though ideally only around right-hand bends.

A later development was the microcar, a movement again spearheaded by the Germans. After the war car-building materials were in short supply, but a job lot of leftover cockpits from the Messerschmitt and Heinkel factories were quickly converted into simple runabouts, although shortages meant that none was ever fitted with more than three wheels. As with the earlier combination, any motorcyclist who had survived the cheesecutter experience was permitted to drive one. But again the concept did not really take off, although quite a few turned over.

The car/bike hybrid then stagnated until the year 2000 and the launch of the – German again – BMW C1. This time, however, the philosophy was a winner – a crash-proof scooter designed for just one-up riding and allowing hard-pressed senior officers to cut confidently through the horrific build-up of traffic caused by the now infamous Retreat from Longbridge.

The C1 rider sat in a proper seat with a five-point safety belt and behind a windscreen fitted with a wiper and washer system. Protruding bump-stops protected machine and occupant in the event of a fall, and the whole offered frontal crash protection equivalent to that of a small car. No airbag was fitted, however, and C1 riders were denied parachutes in the belief that they would undermine morale, although a heated seat, sat-nav and ABS were available. In Britain a helmet was mandatory lest the rider should be recognised.

The C1 was simplicity itself to ride, being essentially a twist 'n' go CVT-equipped scooter with additional bodywork. And because the engine was a mere 125cc and limited to 15bhp, full car-licence holders could ride it providing they passed Compulsory Basic Training, basically a programme of indoctrination involving bollards.

Initially, the C1 was seen to wobble around at low speed owing to its high centre of gravity. Later, it was observed cranked over at mini roundabouts and later still abandoned outside a café while its rider recovered from the shell-shock induced by its four-stroke Rotax single.

Overall, though, the C1 was considered the best attempt yet to combine the security of the car with the convenience of the bike, being narrow enough to bypass traffic jams but without the risks associated with earlier two-wheelers. However, some regarded it as a bit poncey. To counter this, BMW also developed a proper 1,100cc motorbike on which riders could still have proper crashes.

IF HE KNOWS, HE'S NOT SAYING ANYTHING

As the subject for an interview, this man does not look at all promising. The survivor of over 100 life-threatening car crashes, he is best described as the strong silent type, bearing the traumas of his unfortunate lifestyle with tight-lipped, unflinching stoicism. Sid – for side-impact dummy, more properly Euro-Sid to distinguish him from the US equivalent – reveals the misery of his life only through the electronic data logger wired up to the 25 or so transducers and accelerometers implanted in his rather unsavoury rubbery body.

He lives and works at the Transport Research Laboratory near Wokingham and his keeper, Adrian Roberts, is evidently very proud of the lad, TRL having played an influential part in Sid's upbringing and Roberts being personally responsible for his thorax. (His record-breakingly untidy office is littered with books on anatomy and creepy bits of dismembered body.) Sid's work involves not testing new cars but, in effect, testing the tests proposed for side-impact legislation. He sits in for you and me at a preview of the accident supposedly waiting to happen to us, giving an uncannily human form to the mass of recording equipment that determines whether our bones would break. The data on which such calculations are based comes from real accident statistics and the grisly business of crash testing with cadavers. Sid has a brother who also works at TRL. His name is Sid, too.

Considering his obvious personality shortcomings, Sid is a remarkably interesting bloke. (A bloke he definitely is, by the way – the shape of his pelvis confirms it.) He was born in 1990 but was conceived back in 1983 when, in a moment of far-sightedness, a working group of some subsection of the European Experimental Vehicles Committee managed to stay awake long enough to recognise the need for a dedicated dummy design to serve Europe's upcoming side-impact laws. Prior to our man there were two different French dummies, an English one and a number of donor organs available for spare-part surgery, such as an abdomen from Holland. Euro-Sid was created, Frankenstein-like, from the most promising bits of his numerous ancestors – well bred he is not – though these days most of the parts are made in Letchworth. The head, however, comes from America, which probably explains his fine cheekbones.

When I met Sid he was slumped on his trolley in the TRL storeroom, head lolling to one side, bits of junk lying in his lap, expression (what there is of it) fixed and uncomprehending. As in the trenches, his life consists of interminable stretches of inactivity interspersed with brief bursts of unimaginable danger. Interpreter Roberts relishes his description of Sid's role in a typical experimental side-impact test, describing the horror within earshot of the wretched mannequin. Actually, he doesn't have any ears.

Like the highlight in some sideshow of the Victorian grotesque, he is wheeled out before the expectant crowd and strapped roughly into the driving seat – he weighs the same as a fully grown male and is 'not helpful', says Roberts. He is then brought to 'life' with a short, sharp electric shock to his sensors, lights blaze, cameras roll, an ominous whirring sound swells as the crash barrier accelerates to 30mph, but Sid, with the iron-jawed dignity of a revolutionary before the firing squad, 'just stares straight ahead'. The impact is at its most punishing on his spring-loaded ribs and pelvis; his head often smashes against the window and a few seconds later Sid is slumped on the passenger seat in eerie silence, his agony downloaded to the grey box of electronics behind him.

He is not actually designed to sustain physical damage – his ribs, for example, flex beyond a point where ours would snap, sensors determining what real bones would do. He once lost a leg in an accident but generally gets off lightly compared with his more distant relatives in frontal impact testing, whose heads have been known to roll around on the floor. A placard around his neck proclaims: 'Lives left: 6/10'. Another six prangs and Sid will be ruthlessly pulled apart by his keepers for recalibration, to ensure his capacity for suffering has not been dulled. He is still young for a dummy; Roberts reckons there are years of alternating neglect and abuse left in him.

Sid's job is a crucial one and he performs it with Samaritan selflessness, absorbing our own pain by proxy and softening the blow if it should ever come to us. And yet I can't help but dislike him intensely. It's something to do with his impenetrable exterior, his spooky sub-humanity, his contemptible *passivity*; make a cruel joke about his missing forearms, slap his face, strap him in a car and crash it, pull his head off even – his expression remains cold, fixed and unrevealing. Such a loveless existence must make an impression somewhere other than in the crash-test log. Like the mild boy who was bullied at school, there is surely only so much even a dummy can take. . . .

I now have a new nightmare in which Sid and all his po-faced friends rise up, take to the roads and exact a terrible revenge.

PART 3 – THESE ONES ARE ACTUALLY ABOUT CARS, SORT OF

HOW GREAT CARS COME TO BE ABANDONED IN OLD BARNS

Every now and then, one of the classic car magazines runs a type of story that has always baffled me. It begins with the revelation that something like a rare Lamborghini has been found abandoned in a garage.

Reading on, we discover that it's been there since 1980. It's very dusty and the tyres are flat but, remarkably, it's complete and in need of only 'gentle recommissioning', as the classics lot put it.

A few months later we see a picture of the same car, gleaming like new, and bowling down a tree-lined road in the hands of a bloke who never imagined he could get his hands on such a thing. Marvellous.

Now here's what I've never understood. How did anyone ever forget about owning a Lamborghini?

Or grow bored of owning one? How did a car that is obviously in sound condition end up sitting idle for 25 years? If the previous owner didn't like it, why wasn't it sold? Or even given away? All it took was a postcard in the local newsagent's window.

I can see how a fountain pen might work its way to the back of a desk drawer and be overlooked for two decades. A few years ago I bought my girlfriend a pair of boots that she didn't really like, and they are in the corner of her wardrobe, still in the original box and awaiting the great day when they appear on eBay as an item of mint and unused retro chic. But a car? I really don't foresee a day when I can't be bothered with my Boxster any more, and I just leave it in its garage gathering mould and mouse droppings. Apart from anything else, I'd want the garage space.

But now I understand exactly how it happens. I recently drove around France making a new pro-gramme for the BBC, and for this purpose I bought a 1989 Jaguar XJ-S convertible.

It was a good one. Everything on it worked, there was no rot, the hood was free of tears, the mileage was confirmed at under 60,000, and I loved it. Before I left I had it thoroughly serviced and checked over, and a few marginal components such as radiator hoses and brake pads were replaced. It still had its original toolkit and spare wheel, and even the unused bag thing that the conscientious owner is supposed to use to cover the hood when it's folded. And I've always wanted an XJ-S convertible.

After a few days of driving around France, it sprang a small oil leak. Tiny, really, and from the little micro switch that governs the oil pressure gauge on the instrument panel. Sadly, this little component was not available in any of the local garages I tried, so I resigned myself to topping up the oil instead. It was only losing a spoonful of 20/50 each day, and as it was all dripping on France I wasn't that bothered. I'd sort it out when I got home.

And this is exactly where all those Lamborghini-in-a-barn stories really begin. The Jaguar had crossed that invisible line between being a car and being a car that 'needs some work'. It was the first scuff on a new pair of shoes, the first chip in the paint of a newly decorated room, that moment when the case for your sunglasses disappears.

So when the air conditioning packed up owing to some otherwise minor electrical fault, I decided to live with it for the moment. The car needed work anyway, so that was just something else to add to the list. As was the passenger-door mirror, which somehow became detached from its electric motor, so that the motor whirred away but the mirror didn't move. I could sort that out in half an hour when I was in my own garage with my own toolbox.

I think you can see where this is going. There were now three faults with the Jag, and fixing them all was probably a day's work. That became two days when a Frenchman drove into the back of me and bent the bumper. And then it needed another day, because another Frenchman (or it may have been a German, since we were in Alsace and no one is entirely sure who owns it at the moment) scraped a rear wheel arch in a car park.

This is why the so-called 'rolling restoration' of an old car never works; the notion that the car can be driven while you complete all those little jobs concerning trim, paint, interior lights, dicky alternators and so on. It's not possible, because in driving the car you will create problems quicker than they can be cured. A rolling restoration is really just a headlong and brakeless descent to the scrapyard.

And as the weeks passed, more things fell apart. The trip computer died, the back of the driver's seat fell off, one of the windows became loose, the exhaust started blowing when I clouted it on a boulder, the radio aerial jammed in the down position.

Here's where it ends. For complex reasons to do with insurance for filming, the Jag was actually bought by the production company making the programme, the idea being that I would buy it from them when we'd finished. I've now put it in their car park and run away, so it could stay there for 20 years. And then a *Classic Cars* journalist as yet unborn will find it and wonder how it came to be forgotten.

I still want an XJ-S, but I don't want that one. It's broken. If I'd mended the oil leak I might have stayed on top of it, but I didn't and now it's ruined. It's been filed under 'too difficult', like the letter from the video hire shop reminding me that I still have their copy of *Where Eagles Dare* and owe them £120. That's been at the bottom of my in-tray for at least six years.

If there's anything wrong with your car – *anything* – stop what you're doing and go and sort it out. Now. Same goes for your house. There's probably a loose door knob or a damp patch that needs fixing. Do it.

Do it, before the next problem comes along, or it will all become too much. It may seem like nothing more than an irritating small job to you, but somewhere, a man with a bulldozer is limbering up for the demolition job.

BREAKING DOWN IS NOT SO HARD TO DO

I've had the AA out five times in the last six months. Once for a motorcycle, twice for the Range Rover, once for the '70s Lamborghini and now for the 911. If I carry on at this rate I'll be blackballed and required to go into the club library with my revolver to do the decent thing.

Most breakdowns are pretty tiresome – flat batteries, wonky starter motors, fuel-pump fuses and what have you. And on the whole they seem to occur when the car isn't even running, which invites comparisons with the old saw about the Christmas tree lights that were working when you put them away.

But the 911's was interesting because it resulted from the failure of a small electronic sensor on the crankshaft, the signals from which are vital to the function of the little computer that ministers to the engine. So when that went, everything packed up. There was no misfiring, no clattering, no precursor of dissent from the workings of the flat six, in fact no warning at all. One moment the 911 was functioning perfectly, the next it wasn't functioning at all.

There must have been an exact point in time, yet occupying no time in itself, that divided the era when the 911 worked from the era when it didn't. It was a good, clean breakdown.

Curiously, I'd been reading Ralph Barker's excellent *Brief History of the Royal Flying Corps in World War 1*. Engine failures were common in early aeroplanes, especially during the full-power stress of take-off, and the correct course of action was (still is, in fact) to pick a field as near to directly ahead as possible and return to earth with the aeroplane in a reusable condition. The wrong course of action was to give in to the impulse to turn back to the airfield, which would usually result in a stall, a spin and a crash.

This bit of early aviation lore served me well on the dual-carriageway portion of the A4 near London. With the 911 suddenly, utterly and irrevocably dead in the outside lane, there were but a few seconds in which to choose a place to land. With just a few mph left on the clock, I rolled safely into the car park of a corporate complex.

Contrast this with the demise of my chum Hammond's ancient MG Midget. That breakdown was such a drawn-out and agonising episode that there was time for us to have an argument about it while it was still happening.

It was an early autumnal evening, the air crisp and damp; just the sort of air, in fact, that a simple carburetted British sports car engine likes to breathe. We bowled along past hedges and ditches, the gleaming road illuminated by the urine-yellow glow of the Lucas so-called 'headlamps'.

A shudder in the bowels of the thing presaged its end. But it was still running, just not quite as vigorously as before. Then another, and irrefutable indications that power was tailing away: the headlamps became even dimmer. 'Fuel pump,' he cried. 'No, no, ignition,' I retorted, above the howling, but diminishing, 35mph slipstream.

Now we were like the crew of a Bristol F.2b Fighter, nursing our crippled kite back to base after an encounter with the Baron. We could turn back to the petrol station where we'd just refuelled, and give ourselves up. Or we could drive on, fortified by the thought of a hot cocoa back at the Hammond mess.

Another lurch, as if the far end of a long rope paid out behind us had snagged on something. And then another. The Midget was clearly doomed and yet refused to go quietly, continuing to rage against the dying of the headlights. If this were a crash there would have been time to ring the insurer and describe the damage as it happened.

Of course, we didn't make it, but this time it was impossible to discern the precise moment when the engine gave out. It simply diminished to nothing, as the sound of a bell does. Like an old soldier, it just faded away.

For the early RFC fliers, battling against a prevailing wind that usually blew east, the risk was always that you'd come down in no-man's land. And now here we were, alone and in the dark, somewhere only marginally less dangerous – rural Gloucestershire.

Still, I like a good breakdown. I like the drama, the tension, the heightening of the senses as you seek through fingertips, buttocks and ears for signs that you might just get 'home. And I like the finality of the silence that comes afterwards, when I sit and await the curling echo that heralds the yellow van of my despair.

LAMBORGHINIS ARE GREAT. YOU SHOULD HAVE ONE.

Little is of less consequence to the car enthusiast or general car consumer than the UK motor industry's sales figures.

I mean, who really gives a stuff? So Jaguar sales are down 19 per cent, and Jaguar is apparently 'in crisis'. But a mate of mine has just bought one and he's chuffed to bits. Aston Martin sales were up 182.4 per cent, which is nice for them, but another mate has bought one of those and he's very cross, because it keeps conking out. Maybach sales were down 26.1 per cent, but should that put the prospective buyer off? Of course not. There are far better reasons for not having one, such as a Rolls-Royce Phantom (up 7.1 per cent).

I am indebted to *Autocar*, a magazine that once fired me, for the brightly coloured bar chart currently laid out on my desk. And although it is really of relevance only if you happen to own a car factory, it's strangely compelling reading. For example, last year 18,137 of you came up with a presumably sound reason for buying a Chevrolet-nee-Daewoo, or Chevrolaewoo, which is 18,137 more reasons than I can muster. Elsewhere, I am surprised to learn that 1,281 UK residents bought a Ssangyong in 2005. I'm not sure I've ever seen a Ssangyong.

But here's the thing I find really shocking. UK Lamborghini sales were down 56.9 per cent in 2005. This is a tragedy.

Now. I realise that percentages are dangerous and misleading, and that in a sales operation as small as Lamborghini's, a few cars one way or the other are going to make a bigger percentage difference than they would at Ford (whose Focus remained the nation's favourite, topping the table with *shut up*). We're talking here about total sales of 78, which means one extra Gallardo out of the door would represent an increase of 1.3 per cent, or better than Mercedes-Benz managed in 2005 despite selling 82,247 cars. See what I mean?

On the other hand, it still means that there were 100 fewer Lambos ushered out on to Britain's roads last year than there were in the year before, and that means 100 cars not available for small boys to point at and chase on bicycles. And that's not right.

My experiences with Lamborghinis have not been good. After 25 years of waiting, I finally drove the legendary Countach, pin-up of my boyhoood bedroom wall, and hated it with every fibre of my battered buttocks and bleeding eardrums. My Uracco disintegrated. The Diablo I borrowed was pink and became stuck in a side road. By the time we arrived at the Murcielago, Lamborghini had become the geography homework of my motoring education, and I simply didn't bother.

Nevertheless, a Lamborghini remains my favourite of all the supercars I wouldn't buy. Nothing brightens up my day quite like spotting a Lamborghini, not least because it will probably be orange or lime green.

I can't help but have a sneaking regard for the sheer effrontery of these things. Ever since the 350GT of 1964, Lamborghini has been baring its bottom at Ferrari and singing nah nah nah nah nah, and has become the perfect antidote to all that tiresome old toot about race breeding and *passione*.

Everyone knows Feruccio Lamborghini was a tractor maker turned bad. There's an apocryphal story that he bought a Ferrari and thought he could do better; the truth – and I heard this from someone who knew him – is that the clutch burned out on his Ferrari and he asked one of his tractor mechanics to replace it. The spanner man later entered his office with the new component, pointing out that it was exactly the same as the one in their tractors but cost 10 times as much. Lamborghini then realised that he'd make more money from selling supercars to playboys than he would flogging mechanical horses to horny-handed sons of honest agrarian toil.

So a Lamborghini is an upstart, a pretender. But it's a bit like Charles Kennedy, in that we're obliged to disapprove but, secretly, we quite admire him. Ferraris are too often owned by uptight people who attribute great significance to some overtaking manoeuvre that occurred in a grand prix back in 1969. Rod Stewart bought a Lamborghini, just as soon as he'd finished shopping for some leopard-skin trousers and hair product.

There are 100 like-minded people out there who didn't do the decent thing in 2005. Shame on you. I don't want a Lambo, but I want you to have one so that I can see it and smile.

I feel about Lamborghini the way I feel about the Salvation Army. I'm not a member, and I don't especially want anything to do with them. But I still like to think all that stuff is going on.

PIOUS PORSCHE PEDDLES PATHETIC PEDAL-POWERED PRODUCT

Once upon a time, you rode a bicycle because you were either poor or still 12. Cycling was a simple matter back then: you bought a bicycle because it was the only way of getting around.

Today, of course, things are much different. Cycling has long since been hijacked as a socio-political movement by militants, and I know this because I was sitting in my local Chinese the other day, watching the stream of bicycles going past the window.

They were all being ridden not so much by people who needed to be somewhere but by people who wanted to draw attention to themselves. How can I be so sure? Because they were all in fancy dress, and you only appear in public in fancy dress because you're trying to make a statement. It's why the Fathers for Justice always turn up as Spiderman.

Unfortunately, the cyclists' statement seemed less compelling than the fathers'. It seemed to be either (a) I am an eco warrior of greater moral rectitude than you or (b) I'm stupid enough to spend £75 on an item of headwear that anywhere else would be regarded as a disposable medium for the shock-free transportation of television sets.

As someone who still enjoys a good bike ride, I'm saddened by this sort of thing. But then I saw something even more alarming. A chap pedalled past on a Porsche bicycle.

I'd completely forgotten that Porsche made bicycles. In one sense, of course, there's nothing remarkable about it. The motor industry has always owed an incalculable debt to the bicycle, not least because it was the bicycle that gave ordinary people a taste for the personal liberty that led naturally enough to the desire for cars.

More significantly, countless car companies began life as cycle makers and only gradually progressed, often via motorcycles, to cars; in fact, there are few that don't have a rusty bicycle somewhere in the back of the corporate shed.

But I've decided that the only car makers who should be allowed to make bicycles today are those with an uninterrupted history of doing so. And the only one that would appear to qualify is Peugeot.

What, exactly, is Porsche achieving by dabbling in bicycles? It would be tempting to think that with their expertise in manufacturing and their knowledge of new materials, they would be well placed to raise the state of the bicycle-making art. However, a quick trawl through the bicycle media suggests that Porsche bicycles are entirely conventional. All they have done is raised the state of the art of bicycle pricing: the most basic Porsche, the 'Bike S', costs £1,200, while at the top of the range is the Bike R Dura Ace, which is £3,900 and made of carbon-fibre.

This is the first thing that bothers me. Carbon fibre has become so hackneyed that people are making briefcases out of it, and for no other reason than that they can. It's nothing more than high-tech tinsel, and for a leading car maker to produce a perfectly conventional bike made from an exotic material is a bit like Hotpoint launching a titanium mangle.

What am I to make of a man who rides a lightweight Porsche bicycle? Obviously he's not interested in exercise, or he'd have bought a heavy one. Why not buy some lightweight carbon-fibre dumbbells, or pay a cub scout to go jogging for you? Again, I am forced to conclude that he's drawing attention to himself.

But, as the marketing people might say, the message his bike sends out is the wrong one. There are a lot of people out there who are riding bicycles because they have no choice. Norman Tebbit's dad, for example. For a car maker like Porsche to produce an exclusive £3,900 bicycle is rather rubbing his nose in it. It's a bit like a member of the *That's Life* team spending the night in a cardboard box and claiming to understand the plight of the homeless.

This is what really annoys me about clever-dick car makers' bicycles. They're actually not clever at all. Given the luxury of being able to charge £3,900, anyone should be able to build a good bike. Much more impressive is what Dawes and Raleigh does; that is, building good-quality and perfectly usable mountain bikes for a few hundred quid. For the same reason, the Mazda MX-5 is ultimately a greater engineering and commercial achievement than a £250,000 supercar.

All things considered, the best bicycle in the world is still my Brompton folder. It rides remarkably well for a bike actually designed to collapse, and it folds up much smaller than other folding bikes. It does what any bicycle does, and then something else as well, and is yours from around £370.

Incidentally, Brompton have never made a car. A part of me wishes they would.

THE FOLLY OF TRYING TO SAVE FUEL

I feel I should begin with an apology. On one end of my desk is a large blue folder marked 'reply to these', and in it are all those letters you've sent me over the last few months. Hundreds of the buggers. And, in contravention of my usual policy of accountability and openness, not one has gone answered.

I'm very sorry. I've been busy, I let it build up a bit too much and then it sort of got away from me. I don't have any envelopes and I'll need to buy hundreds of stamps, and since the 24-hour petrol station at the end of my road closed down, I don't know where to get them.

But I'll do it eventually. In fact, I can make a start now with a letter from Phil Snook, who I've just realised was the biology teacher at my sixth-form college. His question concerns petrol consumption.

Which is the more economical way to drive in town, he wonders: to accelerate briskly between sets of red lights so that you spend longer with the engine merely idling, or to drive gently between them, which would mean less time spent at the next lights but more time working the engine?

Well, I like a bit of amateur physics and I think I know the answer to this one. The fact is – and it's one on to which most motorists have failed to cotton – that *braking consumes petrol*. In essence, the brakes work by converting the kinetic energy of the car (i.e. that which it has through motion) into heat at the brake discs. Maybe also a bit of heat in the tyres as well, if you've overdone it.

If you overdo it a lot and hit a tree, some of the kinetic energy of the car will be converted into noise and an inflated insurance premium. But either way it has to go somewhere because, as we know from Newton, it cannot be destroyed.

It cannot be created, either. So the kinetic energy of the car must have come from somewhere, and that somewhere is the petrol, which has energy locked in it waiting to be released by combustion and converted to motion through pistons and gears and what have you. So if you're thinking of braking heavily, maybe you should consider simply emptying a bit of your fuel tank on to the road and setting fire to it. At least you won't be wearing out the brake discs.

Therefore the most economical way to drive between the traffic lights is to accelerate at such a rate that the next set will have changed to green just before you get to them, thus removing the need to brake at all. And there you have it. I believe that was a lot easier than some of the questions we used to ask Mr Snook about 'biology'.

Unfortunately, this brings up a rather more sensitive question, namely, should we worry about saving petrol anyway? I think not.

Every time I do the arithmetic I come to the conclusion that saving petrol is pointless. I know we now have some of the most expensive gravy in the world, but the cost of it still amounts to a hill of beans compared with the real cost of owning a car.

This is true even of a supposedly depreciation-proof classic, as I have proved through scientific experiment with my old Bentley. It does 14mpg, and then only if I drive like an undertaker, which makes it quite expensive to use. But maintaining it has ruined me, so the only real route to better economy is to get rid of it altogether. Trying to drive it economically would be fatuous.

So the old adage that says 'if you can't afford the fuel you can't afford the car' is probably as true as it was when it was coined, which was when four-star cost three-and-six and most British people only had one pair of shoes.

Here's what I honestly think. If you're the sort who regards motoring as a necessary evil, don't try to drive economically. Just buy a truly economical car, since they're generally cheap to buy and maintain as well, and drive normally. If you're a car enthusiast, forget the cost of fuel. Worrying about it is like an alcoholic drinking less to save money.

Trying to save fuel is a truly false economy, and for proof of that consider WO Bentley himself. He advised that you should 'drive as if your brakes had failed', which I always took to mean 'drive in a gentlemanly fashion'. But now I suspect he was just trying to eke an extra few mpg out of a Speed Six.

And what good did that do him, eh? A few years after he wrote that, he went bust.

JEREMY CLARKSON RUINED MY DREAM CAR

Regular readers will know that I'm a great fan of inventing new games with my TV colleague, TV's Richard Hammond. One of my favourites is called Airport Shopping Dare, and here's how to play.

It's really very simple. When you're at the Heathrow departure terminal with a chum and a few hours to kill, you will inevitably abandon every tenet of real manhood and end up walking around the shops together. Now you must spot something you think the other bloke could be persuaded to want and then, through subliminal psychological torture, force him to buy it. Nothing too elaborate, usually, just daft T-shirts, sunglasses, that sort of thing.

There really is no feeling more satisfying than being responsible for making a good mate look like a total pillock at his own expense. And I'm pretty good at it. My best result to date is cajoling Hammond into buying a pretty expensive wristwatch with the money he would be earning the following week from opening an orphanage or something. Soon afterwards he got me back with a brown jacket that makes me look like a driving instructor.

But this week I've had my best game of Airport Shopping Dare ever. It wasn't actually played in an airport but a Lamborghini dealership, and this time I was with my other TV colleague, TV's Jeremy Clarkson.

Now, Clarkson has decided he rather likes the Gallardo Spider. I rather like it too; the difference, though, is that he might consider chopping in his Ford

GT for one. He certainly would, I decided, if I had anything to do with it.

And that bit wasn't too difficult, because he clearly wanted one already. I could point out that his new book was selling very well (unlike mine) and that he had earned, both financially and morally, the right to a new Lamborghini. In fact making him buy the thing was clearly a job for a Shopping Dare amateur.

So now the game took a new twist. Clearly he didn't need persuading to buy the car, but he would need to be steered, gently and subtly, into buying it in the right colour scheme. Orange, ideally, or that new '70s bathroom-suite blue they're doing. Either of these would combine quite nicely with a neutral sort of interior leather. Cream, perhaps, or maybe even plain old black.

Jeremy, however, got it into his head that the car would look right in dark green, black, or something called black/green. This he would combine with an interior in orange perforated leather.

And I know what he's thinking of. He's thinking of those Paul Smith brogues that are dark and accountanty on the outside but lined in lime green; respectable and restrained at a casual glance, but revealing a sense of gay chromatic abandon to anyone who gets close enough to see inside. Or maybe it's one of those dinner suits by Ted Baker: completely uniform (as a dinner suit should be) in normal use, but revealing a tantalisingly enigmatic purple lining when removed and cast aside in a moment of attempted seduction.

But we're talking about a Lamborghini here, and this isn't how it's going to come across, in my view. I think it's going to be like a merchant banker who wears a grey suit with a 'funny' Homer Simpson tie. Or an Information Technology professional who wears a grey suit and has a sign above his desk saying, 'You don't have to be mad to work here' and so on. Or a senior hospital administrator who wears a grey suit and says, 'Leave a massage' on his answering machine.

The whole point of a Lamborghini, as we've explained ourselves many times, is that you want one because you're not interested in buying into racing heritage or thoroughbred provenance. That's for Ferrari and Maserati owners. Lamborghini is a bit of an upstart, and you have to demonstrate that you realise as much. A black one suggests that you believe in it, which would be ridiculous. Lamborghinis are a bit vulgar and as such should be celebrated openly with something like the orange. Or that bathroom-blue. But he just didn't get it.

And this is what surprises me. Jeremy is a self-styled champion of vulgarity. I happen to know that he has a very large television set, for example, and electronic garden gates. He goes to footballers' parties and once boasted of going to London's 'biggest restaurant'. But here he is, on the verge of acquiring the automotive medallion of gauche, and he's suddenly concerned about drawing too much attention to himself.

But no worry, because, as with most posh car showrooms, the Lamborghini one provided a selection of painted metal strips and upholstered squares with which the discerning customer can experiment with colour combinations before signing the order form. Playing with these is a pretty good game in itself, and almost as much fun as trying on the frames in Specsavers.

So, out of interest, I tried the green/black paint with the orange leather. It was awful. It made me think of coffee mugs with 'world's greatest golfer' written on them, or 'amusing' doorbell chimes. On the other hand, the orange paint with the creamy pale perforated leather looked like the colour scheme of a man who didn't give a bull's arse about what other people thought, and this, I decided, was what Jezza should have.

So I gathered them up and dived between him and the salesman, waving them around. But he snorted, and then continued talking to the dealer about the price of the cup-holder option.

So I tried the bathroom-blue paintwork with a dark-blue plain leather, which I can assure you would look utterly glorious. Again I approached the man with the Bang & Olufsen mobile, only to be dismissed because he was deep in conversation about service intervals.

In desperation, I even tried white paintwork with the black leather. I found him discussing residual values. I really do think the man may have lost it entirely and turned into an executive.

This is the first time I've ever failed at this game with someone I know well. I have a recurring dream in which Jeremy is on fire and I have the fire extinguisher but can't get the pin out. Even so, I can't stand by and watch him buy the wrong Lamborghini.

So it's over to you. Write to Jeremy at the *Top Gear* magazine address. You don't even need to include a letter. Just remember to mark your envelope, 'James is right, as usual.'

THE RANGE ROVER OF OUTSTANDING
NATURAL BEAUTY

Today, from the window of my office, I have an uninterrupted view of my 1992 Range Rover Vogue SE. I think it may be the sort of thing WB Yeats had in mind when he wrote of 'All things uncomely and broken, all things worn out and old'.

In case you weren't reading two years ago, or you have since found something more interesting to contemplate, I should explain that the Rangey was bought in strict accordance with my principle that one's biffabout car should not cost more than £1 per cc of engine displacement. Not the mintiest Range Rover in the world, then, and definitely not the most aromatic.

And I have never neglected a car quite like I have Old Stinker, which sits there looking positively doleful as I walk on by, averting my eyes from its cack-encrusted flanks and the pastie wrappers piled on the dash and visible through the windscreen. I'm beginning to believe that everything I have ever taken into the Range Rover is still in there, and that includes a bootful of old building materials that I was supposed to take to the dump several months ago. Trouble is, the Range Rover *is* the dump, and if I parked it with the windows open it would soon, like any other skip left around here, be full of my neighbours' garden rubbish.

This is most uncharacteristic. I carry a Hoover around in the Bentley, just in case, and I keep a small, stiff paintbrush in the Porsche for removing dust from those little crevices around the switches. When I drive the Boxster I adjust the air vents and heater controls not for my own comfort, but so that the overall arrangement is symmetrical. I also polish my shoes and wash up while I cook. I can't stand muck, filth and disorder, and yet I've somehow allowed the Range Rover to become completely feral.

One reason for this is that it offers a welcome opportunity to escape the rigours of modern urban life and roll about in my own ordure like Neanderthal man. This office is somewhat similar: an oasis of dirty cups, empty beer bottles, waste paper and general squalor in an otherwise spotless household, like a dog's egg in the middle of a croquet lawn. But there's a better reason for treating the Range Rover in a way that, if it were my cat, would land me in the clanger.

You see, this five-owner, 110,000-mile car is an utterly dependable old bus that I would happily drive to Australia tomorrow, and in the certain knowledge that I would get there. It has never, ever failed me. Of course, this being an old product of Land Rover, lots of little things have gone wrong with it, but here's the weird thing: they always mend themselves.

At first, I thought I was imagining this, but it's happened so many times now that I have to acknowledge something is going on. Items that you would get a garage to attend to but for which I have allowed nature to take its course have included a broken fan, two broken electric windows, the air conditioning, the air suspension controls, the headlight main beam switch, one of the seat motors, the rear windscreen wiper, the rev counter, the central locking and a slow puncture.

I swear I'm not making this up. In fact, it's beginning to give me the creeps a bit. Yesterday, a light bulb had blown in the instrument panel. Today, it glows like the star of David. If I go anywhere near this thing with a spanner or a screwdriver it immediately crosses that invisible line that separates the merely poorly from the dead. But if I leave it alone it eventually recovers. It's a bit like having a spot. Squeeze it and you will be left with a scar, but leave the job to time's patient skill and eventually it will disappear, leaving you with a completely unblemished nose. If I drive the Range Rover when several things are not working I can feel that it's slightly out of sorts, because some of its qi energy is being directed to the task of healing.

And to think that the occasional sandalled leftist has scrawled 'climate crime' and 'environment nazi' on its heavily soiled bonnet. Nothing could be more inappropriate, since what I have in my Range Rover is the world's first organic and alternative therapy vehicle; a truly living machine with the antibodies to mechanical ague coursing through its metal metabolism. It is, in fact, the most ethically correct, GM-free and plain greenest vehicle I have ever come across.

I mean it: if I leave it alone for a week, things grow on it.

POETRY ON MOTION

People of Britain, put aside your concerns over the cleanliness of hospitals, Gordon Brown's plans for public spending and trying to remember the name of the Liberal Democrats bloke. This election drudgery is of no more consequence than the captaincy of the local bowls club when set aside the great dénouement that awaits you here; namely, the final and incontrovertible resolution of the Great Sports Car Debate.

I salute you, readers of *Telegraph Motoring*. Some weeks ago I asked you to settle a debate that has reverberated through lounge bars across the land for three generations: what, exactly, and in no more than 12 words, is the definition of a sports car? At stake was the future custody of a 1/43rd-scale die-cast model of a Mazda MX-5 that has sat on the windowsill of my office for the last six years.

To be honest, I expected a handful of old biffers to write in about the Austin Healey 3000, and indeed they did. One of them even apologised. But there was more. From every corner of these sceptered isles the pithy missives flooded in; my letter-opener is like the bread knife in a busy sandwich bar, burnished and flashing in the morning sun, worn to half its original depth by the unrelenting slicing action of over 450 openings.

I have to say, though, that simply sending in the name, or even a picture, of your own car is not really good enough. On the other hand, Ms Hanya Gordon made it straight to the shortlist by including a bag of American Hard Gums, while anyone who had the temerity to dismiss my old 911 was immediately filed under 'B'.

There was a man who called me a big jessie for not buying a TR6, a man who said 'sports car' was a contradiction in terms, some misleading stuff about driving gloves and bonnet straps, and quite a bit of chicanery involving complex phrases that formed the acronym SPORTSCAR. The crossword is on the back of the main paper.

There was whimsy from old ladies who yearned for the bark of a straight six and the glint of a wire wheel glimpsed with an expectant twitch of a curtain, and there was baser stuff from young men revolving around things that are or aren't possible in the cockpit of an MG. It is famously said that 40 per cent of American marriages are proposed in a car, but it seems that the British are keen to dispense with these stuffy and outdated formalities. Holly Burns of Glasgow sent me a treatise of mediaeval density and including some French words, which is no good to a man who needs something to remember for the pub, while the brevity consolation prize goes to Mike Coward of Southport, who said that a sports car is 'yee-haaa'. But then, so's square dancing.

I liked the suggestion of Reg Santer, from Horsham, that 'a sports car is all in the mind', until I realised that he was playing into the hands of manufacturers who claim sportiness for their mini-MPVs. Maurice Davies almost won with 'A Don Quixote story fused to an engine' and Paul Smith of Kendal seemed close with 'One being driven faster than it ought to be'. But then I realised that this would be true of a Kia Rio in any situation.

There was the philosophical, such as Anthony Marshall of Barnsley with 'a state of mind with wheels but without remorse or thought'. The snappy: 'one designed to go from A to A', according to Peter Gardner of St Albans. And the foreboding, from Mike Peers of Henley: 'Every man's dream, few men's reality, and every mother's nightmare.' Then again, I had a girlfriend like that.

You see, it's difficult, which is why this debate has raged for so long. But when I read that a sports car is 'An ode to joy/on open road,/Wind in face,/Grin like Toad' I realised that the poet's skill with imagery was needed to define it in 12 words or fewer. Here's Hamish Kidd, possible former lyricist with Wham:

Free as air
Wind in hair
Heel 'n' toe
Let's go
Brrrm brrrm!

Or, drawing heavily on Spike Milligan, Ian Hourston of Orkney:

A sports car is
A car with fizz
Forget your quiz
It's simple, viz:
A whiz.

And Bill Richardson of Guisborough, apparently a student of Hilaire Belloc:

A powerful engine in a saucy shell,
Built to go like bloody hell.

But I thought I'd stumbled upon an undiscovered fragment of Ted Hughes when I opened an offering that defines nothing precise about the sports car yet somehow captures its essence completely. The winner is Alan Lidmila of Sheffield with 'The floored howl, dawn clear undulating blacktop wheel-gripped view ahead.'

That should silence the car bores in my local.

ONLY THE FRENCH WOULD BUILD A CAR DESIGNED TO BREAK DOWN

I've spent the last week driving a car with a bad battery, a dicky charging circuit and a less than reliable starter motor.

Come to think of it, I've spent much of the last 20 years driving cars like this and, to be perfectly honest, it's bloody boring. Few things in life are more useless than a car that won't start, so if its ability to do so is in any doubt, the best thing to do is leave it running.

All those years of jump leads and bump starts have scarred me. Every time I shut a car down, even a new one, a part of me wonders if it's going to start again. Irrational, I know, but to me it's rather like that sound of a car horn at the beginning of the Stones' 'Honky Tonk Women'. I've heard it a thousand times, but every time it comes on the radio in the car I look around to see who's beeping at me.

For this reason, I won't be test driving the new Citroen C2 'Stop&Start', a car that turns itself off every time it comes to a halt in the interests of the environment. Even if you simply pause at a zebra crossing, it cuts out. I'd be a bag of nerves.

I know, because around 10 years ago I tried something similar in the form of the VW EcoGolf, I think it was called. This was a normal Golf with a whopping battery and some rudimentary electronic controller that killed it at traffic lights and then fired it up anew when you pulled away. On a technical level, it seemed to work quite well. On a mental one, it was like a form of psychological torture used by an oppressive regime;

the sort that destroys a man's mind without leaving any visible wounds. I write as someone who recently completed a 300-mile journey in an old car without stopping the engine once, even during lunch and a short afternoon nap.

What, in any case, is the point of all this? Making a car that knows when to turn itself off can't be easy, and I suspect that thousands of Citroen's engineering man-hours have been devoted to the problem when they could have been better spent hunting down and despatching whoever was responsible for the Pluriel.

But no doubt someone, somewhere, has done a calculation to show that if every engine in Britain stopped for a few seconds at every junction we could reduce CO_2 emissions by a billion tons a year, or something like that. This sort of thing is beginning to annoy me. We've had the one about turning the telly off instead of leaving it on standby, and sooner or later I'm going to calculate what reduction in CO_2 could be achieved if every driver in the country saved a little vehicle weight by removing the owner's handbook from the glovebox. With so many cars, televisions, refrigerators and boilers in the land, it's easy to turn innocent human fallibility into some sort of climate crime.

Beer, for example, must be destroying the planet. If you drink beer, as I do, you have to get up in the night for a wee-wee. That means turning the light on and consuming a tiny bit of electricity. Negligible, really, but if every adult male is doing it, it can be shown to equate to another X tons of pollutant in the air.

Rambling is especially selfish. If you walk for 20 miles, I imagine you build up an enormous appetite.

This means using more gas or electricity to cook more food, and places a greater demand on the refrigeration at Sainsbury's. Since the Ramblers are one of the biggest organisations in the country, this must mean that stomping around in a kagoul is blighting the lives of our children.

And so it goes on. It would be interesting to know how much CO_2 is being produced by the computers of environmentalists who generate fatuous statistics.

The facts are these. There is a finite supply of fossil fuel left and, in broad terms, consuming it is going to create the same amount of pollution. It doesn't matter whether I drive the Bentley and use it all up tomorrow, or drive something that conks out temporarily at every junction and eke it out for another few years. Conserving energy is ultimately fruitless and, more to the point, completely at loggerheads with the demands of a progressive world.

So – and assuming that fossil fuel consumption really is an issue – here's a suggestion. All the endeavour and ingenuity, all the time, equipment and resources, all the wit and learning; in short, every manifestation of human effort being wasted on the C2 Stop&Start, the hybrid, the wind farm and the ecological washing machine – it should all be directed towards finding the alternative.

THESE MODERN SUPERCARS ARE ALL BLOODY RUBBISH YOU KNOW

Not so long ago, driving a Ferrari or a Porsche would have invited accusations of being a right tosser. This was possibly fair enough, since the culture of the time said that anyone who took cars that seriously was probably a bit of a saddo.

Porsche and Ferrari have always taken themselves terribly seriously. Porsche bang on about 'excellence' and Ferrari about 'passion', as if they're the guardians of the proper expression of these conceits of the human condition. But it's all cant, really. Excellence is more important in the manufacture of synthetic heart valves, and passion manifests itself more properly in the bedroom. Attempting to express these things through one's choice of car was perhaps indicative of a few problems in the trouser department.

And how unimaginative was it, if you suddenly found yourself a bit flush, to go and buy a 911 or an F360? The 911 was like the Hugo Boss suit of the successful executive, and choosing a Ferrari was as hackneyed as the expression 'just like mamma used to make' in the description of lasagne in an Italian restaurant menu. Thinking people would think of something a bit more original.

But something strange has happened. All of a sudden, the 911 and the F430 are what the clever people are buying. What were for so long clichés are now rising from a mire of confused car culture like swords of truth. Crikey.

I'm not going to claim that everything's rosy. There's still far too much tasteless Ferrari merchandise for my liking, and far too much talk of the significance of Formula One. These people are claiming that the F430 was developed using the computer 'normally reserved for Michael Schumacher's racing car', but this is obviously bollocks. Why would they do this? Does Michael Schumacher not let other Ferrari people use his stapler?

And the 911 isn't entirely in the clear, because Richard Hammond has just ordered one, and he uses hair product. But even so, the 911 and F430 are suddenly very cool.

One reason for this is that people are once again taking cars very seriously. They may be portrayed as the biggest threat to society since Hitler, and we may be encouraged to feel guilty about them and to want a small diesel hatchback, but deep down people are very, very switched on to what makes a great car. I cannot remember a time when so many people have wanted to engage me in highly informed conversation about cars and what they're like. And I don't just mean the bores from my local; I'm including people like my neighbour Ben, who pinned me against the wall for a good half hour to talk about a Mercedes Benz he'd been looking at, even though he can't drive. And earlier this year I discovered that my mother understood the effect of low-profile tyres on ride and handling.

If we're going to take cars seriously, we need serious cars. Some serious cars that spring to mind are the Bentley Arnage T, the Fiat Panda, the Vauxhall Astra VXR, the Lexus GS430 (no, really), the Citroen C6 and the Renault Grande Espace. In the arenas in which they compete, they do what they're supposed to do

with conspicuous thoroughness, to the enduring satisfaction of the intelligent and informed owner.

It's the same with the 911 and the F430. They're
superb cars that work brilliantly, and in this day and
age that's what matters once again.

Viewers will remember that we had the 911 up
against the BMW M6 and the Aston V8 on the Isle of
Man a few weeks back. I was expecting to go for the
Aston, but after a few hundred miles I realised that the
911 was still a better car. It's always difficult to explain
what makes a 911 great; in fact, on first acquaintance it
feels decidedly wonky. The driving position is still
slightly odd and old-fashioned, and the engine is still
ostensibly in the wrong place. But once it gets under
your skin – and it will – it's there for good. Maybe there
is something in heritage, bloodline and all that other
guff that Porsche would put forward in the showroom.

There certainly is where Ferrari is concerned. There's
more utter cock talked about Ferrari than about any
other subject on earth, even football. But there is
something about a small V8 Ferrari that cannot be
found in any other car. It's not mystique or any of that
nonsense. It's because it works, brilliantly.

When we took the F430, the Zonda and the Ford
GT to France, I became unutterably convinced of this.
The Fezza is the connoisseur's choice, the one that the
true lover of cars and driving will appreciate the most.
Surely it's no coincidence that the F430 is the product
of a company that has been devoted to the supercar
cause for decades?

You simply cannot fake this stuff. Other makers
seem to imagine that they can leap straight into the

realm occupied by Porsche and Ferrari with some ludicrous performance figures, seductive styling and a bit of savvy marketing. But some of us know better. Other cars may be more fashionable, but look beyond that and you will discover that the others aren't actually as good at being great cars.

But here's what really amazes me. The Porsche and the F430 no longer look ostentatious. Every other expensive sports coupe or supercar has become so bound up with bling and football that these two are now appearing to go quietly amidst all the fuss. The latest 911 is one of the most subtly beautiful yet, but remains workmanlike and discreet. The interior is superbly assembled yet is still, above all else, entirely functional, whereas the Aston's interior is disappointing in its details and smacks of flim-flam.

The F430 is clearly still a touch flamboyant, especially in spider form, but it is inoffensively styled. It's more like a perfectly turned ankle than a pumped-up cleavage. Compare it with the Zonda thing that Hammond was driving in France. It's covered with bits of carbon fibre, which is now the Burberry check of the supercar world. It's all tinsel and has nothing to do with the joy of driving.

Call me old-fashioned, but my first requirement of a cooker is not that it's brushed stainless steel; it's that it roasts joints.

TRACK DAYS, OR THE FUTILITY OF GOING NOWHERE

The other day, I and my two *Top Gear* colleagues had a bit of a race. The venue was Castle Combe circuit, the cars were three '70s Italian exotics, and we were deeply embroiled in one of our old-car challenges.

Laps were driven against the clock; there were points won for beating a certain time and points lost for being late. Usual sort of thing.

This much I can reveal. I was last, in an old Lamborghini, and I'm absolutely delighted. I've never been especially good at circuit driving, I have immense difficulty in driving fast and talking to the camera at the same time, and in any case I always end up caring about our old nails too deeply. These are noble and dignified reasons for defeat, and better than the lame snivelling about misfires and wonky brakes that we're used to hearing from the other two.

Better still, the Castle Combe experience helped me to resolve one of the great conundrums of my life as a motoring journalist. Perhaps uniquely amongst my contemporaries, I have never done a track day. And now I've decided that I'm never going to. Never.

For what, exactly, is the point? Apart from the sartorial horror of having to dress up in Nomex overalls and gaily coloured fireproof booties, a track day achieves nothing.

Some of you may be thinking that a track day would make me a better driver. But I'm afraid this is just a rumour put around by advanced driving instructors who run track days, rather in the way that bald men are more virile according to bald men. A race track is not like the real world. There are no pedestrian crossings or bus lanes and all the cars are going in the same direction. I have never driven down the old A40 – one of my favourite roads – to find that someone has thoughtfully placed some fluorescent bollards at the turn-in points for bends. Neither has the local council erected a sign saying BRAKE just before that sharp right-hander near Thame. These are things for me to enjoy working out for myself.

And then there's Frank Melling, *Telegraph Motoring*'s voice of classic motorcycling. He has vowed to take me on a bike track day, but I've decided this is a poor idea as well. I'd probably fall off or end up with a bad dose of Old Bike Face, a skin condition brought on by slavish adherence to classic motorcycling principles and riding through winter in an open-face helmet.

And why would I want to be a better rider? As the marketing people might say, it would be off-message vis-à-vis my core brand values of being a bit useless. If I was any good at riding a motorcycle, all the fear and fun would go out of it. Likewise, if I was good at driving on a circuit, I would be completely redundant at *Top Gear*, where it's my job to be Captain Slow and come last whenever we have a race.

Another school of thought says that track days will reveal something about your car. This much at least appears to be true, since the old Lambo revealed a '70s Malteser. I had braked heavily and rather late for a sudden chicane, or some other track feature with no parallel on real roads and put there purely to annoy me, and saw the fluff-covered vintage confection shoot out from under the passenger's seat. But as I lifted off to turn in (or however these track types articulate the perfectly ordinary business of driving) it disappeared again. I haven't seen it since.

Elsewhere, the rear-view mirror fell off on a left-hander and hit me in the face, and my mobile phone disappeared down one of those crannies 'twixt seat and console designed to admit a mobile phone but not an adult hand. Remarkably, they knew how to do this even in 1975. And under the passenger seat of every car there is, somewhere on the seat-sliding mechanism, a huge blob of thick and filthy grease. This is found on brand-new cars and I can now confirm that it's still there 30 years later, awaiting the moment when someone has to retrieve his wallet after a track day.

Few things in life are more futile than a track day. It is an affront to the liberty and independence offered by the car – not to mention the awesome achievements of the world's tireless road-builders – to wantonly drive in such a way that you will, inevitably, end up exactly where you started one minute thirty-nine point two five seconds later and needing some new tyres.

Or, worse, wedged between some old ones and needing a whole new car.

CLASSIC CARS – YOU HAVE BEEN WARNED

The world is full of misty-eyed optimists. If it wasn't, there wouldn't be a classic car scene. As it is, there is a very big one, and a whole rack of WH Smith's devoted to throwing away money that could have been spent on something useful, such as a new car.

Don't get me wrong – I love old cars. They're fascinating, they're great material for pub debates, and they're endlessly amusing. But I am a man who has gone carpetless for love, while other people imagine they can enter lightly into a relationship with an old car without realising that these things are the Heather Mills of motoring.

Every now and then I receive a letter from a reader or viewer who is interested in buying a classic car and is seeking advice. There has also been a rash of articles in the motoring press recently, headbanging that old chestnut about buying a supercar for Mondeo money, which is becoming so fatuous that it's high time somebody pointed out what a nice Mondeo you could buy with all the money you'd lose on that Jensen Interceptor. Finally, it's almost summer, when people forget the horrors of poor demisting, sticky heater valves and damp starting, and imagine that a Maserati Bora can not only recapture a glorious age of driving freedom but can even be used outdoors.

So here, finally, are the basics: the definitive cut-out-'n'-keep guide to old-car ownership, an executive summary of pending woe that the eternally hopeful can keep in the glovebox. But not the glovebox of a '60s Alfa Spider, because it will go soggy.

Is it vital that you complete your journey?

If so, you need to think about alternative transport arrangements. The most popular solution is something known as a 'modern car'.

Old cars are old

I bought my Bentley T2 with the attitude: 'It may be old, but it's still a Bentley.' The truth is more like: 'It may be a Bentley, but it's still old.' Even the most exotic car is still made from car-making materials, and they wear out. I'm guessing that you no longer use any 30-year-old electro-mechanical devices around the home, and that they probably went in the bin during the '80s. How could anyone expect something built by Fiat in the '70s to still work properly? This is why the expression 'good condition for year' is so meaningless in classic car small ads. If the car in question is something like a Datsun 120Y, then the very fact that it hasn't been scrapped means it's in good condition for the year.

Old cars aren't very good

If they were, they would still be in production. Wonky handling, cussed carburettors and poor fuel consumption are not the real issues here, it's the little things that you hadn't realised were so good on your 2002 Ford Focus – the power of the headlights, the effectiveness of the windscreen wipers, the ergonomics of the seats and so on. Remember that the car is a relatively recent phenomenon, and that a '60s British sports car is, in the evolutionary scale of things, the equivalent of an unmodernised 12th-century farmhouse. It will probably smell similar, too.

Could you run a new one?

If not, you probably can't run an old one properly. The value of a Rolls-Royce undoubtedly goes down quite sharply with time, but a graph representing the burden of maintenance goes, if anything, the other way. This is especially true of exotica such as Aston Martins, Ferraris and Lamborghinis. There is no such thing as a 'cheap classic', not when you can buy a new Kia with a £1 deposit.

Only ever buy a good one

If you have enough money to scrape on to the bottom rung of Ferrari 308 ownership – say £15,000 – buy something like a mint Triumph TR6 instead. Since all old cars are essentially rubbish (see above), you might at least have one in good condition. And sorting out a bad car will always cost at least twice as much as buying a good one in the first place. I know shabby is considered chic in some circles these days, but it only really works for overcoats.

Do you read tool catalogues on the lavatory?

If not, you are not a professional mechanic, so you will need to know one. Cultivate the friendship of a local specialist or a versatile under-the-arches repairer. Mine is a late-'60s Nigel with an impeccable service history and a head full of exploded diagrams of Bentley and Jaguar sub-assemblies. His toolbox is bigger than the T2.

A sobering thought

Of all the cars I have owned over the past four years, the cheapest to run, by a country mile, has been my brand-new Porsche.

ACHTUNG! BENTLEY!

In the general revamping of the Rolls-Royce and Bentley factory that has gone on over the last few years, the most obvious change is to the reception area. From the austere '30s facade of its main admin block now sprouts a glitzy vestibule that is pure architectural showbiz.

It's the sort of thing that beardy Bill Bryson will moan about in his next book, *Notes from a Small Automotive Manufacturing Facility*, and it ought not to work, but it does. Tradition and modernity rub shoulders, challenging but ultimately respecting each other. That is the British way and there is no finer example of it than a current Bentley. But there are a few too many Audis in the car park for my liking.

The temptation at this point is to resort to my collection of Commando War Stories in Pictures books and make a few disrespectful allusions to our favourite adversary in the field of human conflict. But let's be a bit more grown-up about this. I like the Germans. I met Dr Ulrich Hackenberg, the new board member for engineering. He is a splendid fellow, a true Bentley enthusiast and someone whom you'd gladly buy a drink if he baled out and landed in your greenhouse. So no war jokes.

But then I entered the lobby and was confronted with a particularly fine study in oils of a Hawker Hurricane shooting down a Heinkel 111, and this got me thinking. I was at Crewe to drive the year-2000 model Arnage, a car that will come with a choice of not just the twin-turbo 4.5-litre BMW V8 installed at launch (now designated a Green Label Arnage, after the background colour of its winged badge) but also the old 6.75-litre turbo V8 as found in two-door Continental Bentleys (Red Label).

During the war, of course, Rolls-Royce – in this very factory, in fact – produced the Merlin engine for the Hurricane, the Spitfire and a host of other kites. BMW, meanwhile, powered the Dornier 217 and the Junkers 188 and later supplied the unitary engine and nacelle assembly for the outstanding Focke-Wulf 190. So the Battle of Britain still rages under the bonnet of this latest Bentley. I'm sorry, but I just can't help it.

A quick briefing. All year-2000 Arnages have improved rear leg and foot room, courtesy of a redesigned bench and a lowered floorpan. Sat-nav is now standard, as are electrically folding door mirrors and speed-sensitive power steering. Externally, differences are few – clear indicator lenses, bigger 18-inch wheels and revised bumpers housing the discreet sensors for the new parking radar. The ground crew have been up all night working on the suspension, too, but we'll come on to that.

The real action begins under the gently shimmering engine cowlings. Strictly, the Crewe V8 would not fit in the Arnage, but with a few simple modifications it slipped in with suspicious ease. Matthew Waterhouse, the project manager, suspects that the original car's engineers were subconsciously considering it when they drew the engine bay. Engineers are like that – a bit of an undisciplined rabble. Engine assembly is now back in-house, where a small team of our brave lads ministers to this awesome 400bhp, 619lb/ft powerhouse.

A few miles on the road are enough to separate the Englander Bentley from the Hun Bentley. The BMW unit delivers 350bhp and 420lb/ft, and an Arnage thus equipped is no slouch. But once I'd driven the Crewe version, I was tempted to say *Not so fast, Fritz.* It's all about delivery. The awesome low-down torque of the Red Label version means that by the time the Jerry version, piloted by the evil Reichsfotographer Paul Von Dubious, has responded to the order *Achtung! Noch ein cog bitte!* I'm already at angels 15 and waiting in the sun.

The Green Label requires a good kick with the old jackboot to extract real performance, but in the Red Label one merely has to curl one's toes inside one's best Jermyn Street brogues and the Bentley rockets to 60mph quicker than you can say *Good God, Ginger's bought it* – 5.9 seconds. It is superb and, apparently, just what the owners asked for.

In truth, the BMW version is still more refined and quieter. The noise in the 6.75 Arnage would cause a few monocles to fall from fanatical Prussian eye sockets, were it found in a Rolls-Royce, which is why this engine won't be making it into the Seraph. But in a Bentley it seems wholly appropriate, especially as improved engine mountings and increased body rigidity have given the engine note a firmer edge and banished the slight lumpiness found in the two-door cars. The Bentley fairly thunders as you push the throttle through the emergency gate etc., etc. Tally ho!

Since we're on rigidity, we'll come back to the undercarriage. I was under the distinct impression that the new Arnage's ride was softer, but Herr Dr Hackenberg tells me, with a sinister chuckle, that it has actually been firmed up a touch. Torsional improvements have allowed a more precise suspension set-up, which actually makes the ride seem more supple through better overall composure. It proves, once again, that what is genuinely good for handling is generally good for ride, too.

The Red Label Arnage is a fantastic motor car and the best thing that Rolls-Royce/Bentley/VW makes. At £149,000 it is a mere £4,000 more than the BMW-engined Green Label variant, a premium well worth paying. Scramble! Another triumph of British pluck over the white-coated German motor-industry machine, then.

Er . . . no. Apparently Obergruppenführer Ferdinand Piech loved this car so much he had to be forced from it at the point of a well-oiled Webley service revolver. It was a true collaborative effort and harks back to what I said at the beginning about tradition and modernity in happy conspiracy. So now, as Churchill said, let us go forward together.

For this Tommy, the war is over.

THE VAUXHALL VECTRA, A REPRESENTATIVE VIEW

Could be on for a new car. The other day, Gav – he's my boss, MD of Vectra Print/Copy – called me into his office and said, 'Jim,' he said, 'you remember tuna wars? Well, now it's toner wars. The opposition are taking cartridges into Europe and we need to regain the initiative. I'm giving you Germany, Jim. I want you to go over there, get a feel for the place, and while you're there I want you to drive Vauxhall's new Vectra. I don't mind telling you this car could play a role in your future, Jim. I want your report by Monday.'

'I know where you're coming from,' I said, grasping the nettle. 'We need to nail down a cohesive policy on European market penetration. The Vectra could be the business tool we need for more rapid response to client toner needs. I'll run it up the flagpole, see which way it blows.' He looked blank, but I guess he's got a lot on his plate.

First impressions, as any on-the-road executive knows, count for a lot. I wear a company tie to build customer confidence; Vectra wears a purposeful, dynamic suit that picks up the Cavalier's baton (Vauxhall's words, those) and runs with it (mine). I couldn't help thinking it looks a bit like a Primera at the back and there are hints of Peugeot in the slightly tapered headlights. Identity is established with the chrome V sign on the grille; individuality is emphasised by two creases that flow up the bonnet and blend into the pointed door mirrors. I reckoned this was pure styling, but the

Vauxhall rep swears it's like that for aerodynamic reasons.

It's a bit bigger all round than my old Cav, too, giving vital gains in interior room, especially in the back. Overall, its more rounded shape strengthens the Vauxhall corporate look, as established by the Astras our account handlers use and Gav's Omega. Should make for an integrated-looking car park and solid corporate identity, for Vauxhall and for us.

Vectra's aggressive go-ahead stance is consolidated with new suspension, based on subframes front and rear. Vauxhall's mission statement was a smoother ride, better handling and less noise, and a better chassis means less driver stress and better business readiness. I drove a competitor's Mondeo 16v, and it showed how my Cavalier has fallen behind with its jittery ride and soggy nose-led handling, especially with 120K on the clock.

There's a full spectrum of engines, including a diesel (I ignored this, as it doesn't complement our sophisticated blue-chip technology image), four-cylinder petrols in 1.6, 1.8 and 2.0-litre capacities, and a 2.5-litre V6. There are hatch and saloon versions with all engines, and an estate is coming next autumn. I made a decisive decision to go for the 2.0 16v SRi hatch, the obvious replacement for my Cavalier and the car appropriate for my grade (18).

It was lunchtime, so I worked my way gently into Vectra with a brief drive to the local McDonalds for *ein quarter pounder mit cheese und a coffee* (I picked up a bit of the language on the school exchange). It's immediately obvious that the interior is a big improvement over the Cav's – more rounded, softer looking, in keeping with the outside. The seats are better, offering two lumbar adjustments and introducing a height variable, but the wheel doesn't move. That's a shortcoming, because in my ideal seat position my knees are splayed a bit and the left one bangs on the cup holder. While we're at it, my coffee cup didn't fit that well, and it seems odd that Vauxhall didn't involve McDonalds in optimising cup-holder parameters.

During my snatched in-car meal I assimilated more nice touches on the interior. The clock is linked to the RDS radio signal and is automatically changed when you drive into Europe or when we switch to summer time and is disseminated with radio and trip computer info via an in-dash display facility. The ventilation system is now by rotary knobs instead of sliders and my car had excellent optional air conditioning, which is an essential accessory in this weather – if you turn up at a customer's with wet armpits (highly likely in this easy-iron polyester shirt) then you might find yourself with a major disincentive in the agent/client interface which no amount of aftershave will rectify.

Back on the road, I had a quick thrash to the autobahn. This engine is basically an ongoing development of my old car's, with Ecotec variable inlet manifolding for wider reaching torque access. It felt a bit slower than the Cavalier despite this. Vauxhall says it does 0–100kmh in 10 seconds, but I reckon I'd be able to beat that. What's more, I can work on my nought to sixties utilising the computer's stopwatch function, which records tenths of a second for this purpose. The Cav did it in eight, according to *Car*

Magazine, and that figure needs to be kept in perspective: two seconds might seem immaterial now, but it'll seem like a long time when you're staring at the 'add toner' warning light on your photocopier control panel with 150 annual reports still to go.

I'll be honest with you, this engine feels a bit old. At really low revs, say when pulling away gently, it grunts and grumbles worse than our fleet manager. It gets a bit rough at higher revs, too, and this becomes apparent on the usual motorway drag. Up to 70mph Vectra is nice 'n' relaxed, but at 70 I'd be doing my competitors a big favour. I work between 90 and the ton, and up there Vectra's engine introduces a bit of a boom to the cabin ambience equation. That's a pity, because wind noise is kept nicely subdued even at three figures and the tyres are quiet even on those Jerry-built concrete surfaces. Later, I had a quick go in the 1.8, and though it's basically the same it feels much nicer – smoother, quieter, more peppy. That's a grade 15 car, though.

Sharp ridges, such as expansion joints, cause a bit of a clang but it's more a noise than a feeling. There's a grittiness in the suspension that complements the rough edge on the engine and spoils Vectra's composure, but overall the ride is like a good sales pitch – firm but compliant. Even at 120 the Vectra stayed stuck nicely on the road, only crosswinds interrupted by lorries causing a slight waywardness. Not so bad that I couldn't steer with my knees and use my hands for vital meeting preparation, though.

But gains that are made on the motorway in time-management are lost if the car can't hack it on the winding stuff. First thing I noticed on a back-road blast was the pronounced castor effect of the steering, which snaps back to the straight ahead very smartly. This weights up the wheel in a turn, giving an impression of meatiness that isn't really there. In a fast bend the steering is more vague than you'd expect – in short, the wheel's writing cheques the front suspension can't honour.

The good news, though, is that it's quicker-geared than the Cavalier, and this does as much as the air con to reduce the incidence of sweaty moments. The car is much better balanced, too. In a hard-charging corner the Cavalier would nose its way soggily to the edge of the road, demanding more lock which was then harder to wind off. Vectra is more neutral, and can be held squealing through long bends at the outside of the adhesion envelope, allowing maximisation of cornering forces at your disposal (my 2.0-litre was better here than the heavier and differently tyred V6). The gearchange is improved too, though it's still not best-case scenario with its rubbery feel and second ratio feels a bit too tall when powering out of tight turns, where the seat base also reveals an inability to manage a major sideways momentum situation. But compared with my Cavalier, vital seconds can be shaved off response times with Vectra, and it's those last few seconds that make the difference between you or someone else closing that sale.

By the end of a hard day I had established a good, pro-active relationship with Vectra. It's more comfortable, roomier and makes a more dynamic executive statement than its predecessor. However, comparison with the Cavalier is not enough to confirm Vectra's business credentials.

I decided to give it to Gav straight on a one-to-one basis. 'Gav,' I said, 'Vectra offers significant improvements over Cavalier but I don't think it moves the goalposts on the overall executive express playing field. Major problem identified is the engine; it's not at the cutting edge. We need to reassess Vectra in the light of a head-to-head comparative shakedown with major rivals with particular reference to Mondeo, Laguna and Xantia, to establish the way forward for most effective market penetration capability. We need to suck it and see.'

And he said to me, 'Jim,' he said, 'you talk complete bollocks.'

I'VE NEVER FELT SUCH A SPANNER

Anyone who thinks that being a racing car mechanic is a swanky wheel-changing job doesn't know his arse from his elbow-jointed extension piece, and that includes me.

There I was, no less a revered spannerist than James May, owner of an allegedly 99-piece chrome-vanadium socket set and best 'specials' bicycle builder of the fifth form, and I was holding a rag. If you were at Donington Park for round 12 of the BTCC you would, I hope, have noticed how brightly the two silver A4 Quattros of Biela and Bintcliffe gleamed in the watery June sunshine.

It probably didn't help that I arrived for my first day as an Audi pit technician, Saturday, precisely half a day late. By then, practice for the first race was over and there was nothing for it but to have lunch in the motorhome – pork fillets with veg and gravy followed by cheesecake, which was excellent. After an hour or so of digestive repose watching Le Mans on the motorhome telly, I finally entered the dark portal of the pits, hoping to have a look at some telemetry or perhaps join the discussion on tyre choice. That was when I was handed the duster and the bottle of wax. After I'd polished the cars, I washed a pile of alloy wheels. I completely missed the second practice session as I was too busy cleaning the garage floor.

Still, the garage is a fascinating place, even when observed from all fours. There's the toolkit – drawer after drawer of beautiful stuff, with every last spanner, socket, ratchet and extension piece allocated a cut-out slot in a cosseting bed of foam. One corner is devoted to a huge, gleaming plinth on which, with the aid of computers, light beams and other black magic, minute adjustments to camber, toe-in and weight distribution can be made. Everything is absolutely spotless, thanks in some small part to me on this occasion.

You should see underneath the car. I crawled under Biela's hoping for a quick nap, but was stunned into wakefulness by the cleanliness of everything. Even the floorpan is polished, the better to prevent dirt sticking to it and making the job of gearbox and engine changing messy. It's not like your road-going A4. There's no underseal for a start, and the alternator and power-steering pumps are driven from the rear diff rather than the engine, to preserve a few vital horse-power; less than half the engine's output is directed to the back, so they only sap that bit of it. That steering pump is an area of concern. The BTCC A4 is geared at a mere 0.9 turns lock-to-lock, and if the pump fails – as it had done a few weeks previously when a stone fouled the drive belt – then the driver is not strong enough to overcome the leverage of the unassisted wheel and ends up in the gravel, as Biela did.

Dinner was roast turkey with all the ancillaries followed by jelly and ice cream, after which I retired to the hotel with the chaps. Now I thought Saturday nights in race season would pass in a stress-relieving riot of drinking, brawling, seducing and sword-fighting, but tonight it was just a few quiet pints in the bar and some talk of racing. That first practice session had been revealing; it was wet, and our boys, with the advantage of four-wheel drive and hence able to move off the dry racing line on to the slippery stuff for overtaking, had been running first and second until the track started to dry out. Then, encumbered by a 65kg weight penalty levied for being too fast last year, they dropped back to 9th and 12th. What we wanted was a wet race.

Next day the sky, scrutinised over several bacon and egg sandwiches, looks promising. At 09.30, 15 minutes before morning warm-up, light rain begins to fall. Biela wants his 'wet' ratios, which means a gearbox change. Panic? No, the job takes only about 12 minutes. An engine change takes an hour and a bit. The 24,000-mile service should take about 45 seconds, then. I am allowed under the car for the final part of the job, bolting the gearbox cover plate on. The socket slips on the shallow nut and I punch myself in the face.

Our chaps are 2nd and 7th in warm-up, but we need more rain. Biela wants the other gearbox back and I'm invited to help, but by the time I've found a pair of heat-resistant gloves, the box is already swapped. I squirm to the rear diff to help fit the tubular prop shaft. There are no bolts – I push a spring-loaded pin home and, with a satisfied grunt, mate the shaft's female end with the diff's pinion. The bloke at t'other end slides the whole thing forward on to the gearbox and the locating pin snaps into place with a faintly unconvincing ping. Is that it? Presumably, as the exhaust is now being dragged over my chest. This simply slots into place – it's still hot – and is retained with a handful of bolts. Everything on the car has a torque setting and the blokes know them all by heart.

As the race approaches, tension builds. I meet the drivers in the garage – can you imagine this happening in prima donna F1? – and what an unlikely pairing they are. John Bintcliffe is small, stocky and bounces around like an excited schoolboy. Frank Biela is lanky and languid, lurking around with a permanent hunted expression on his face, probably because he's usually having a crafty fag where he shouldn't.

When the pit lane opens, half an hour before the start, the excitement palpably intensifies. It's been declared a wet race, allowing us to switch from slicks to wets but not the other way. So we're out on the grid on slicks, hoping. The sky gleams like mercury, but the track is merely damp. Not damp enough. Almost at the instant the first drop hits my face the cry for wets goes up and the world goes mad.

Air tools rattle like small-arms fire; the single big nut on each axle spins; wheels fly in all directions. My job is to roll the slicks across the grass and heave them over the pit wall to waiting arms. The knack is to get the wheel rolling, give it a bounce and then tip it over the wall like a volleyball. At my first attempt I was run over by my own wheel.

I watch the start from a trackside box, the cubbyhole full of computers and telly screens where you expect to see Frank Williams looking po-faced. Beavis and Butthead streak away from 9th and 12th and arrive at the first corner first and second, but I don't really notice this as I'm busy scanning the now deserted grid for signs of the propshaft. *And it's Biela ... from Bintcliffe ... with Al-ain Me-nu in the Renault some way off but looking dangerous.* It stays like that, thanks to steady rain, until the last half of the last lap, when that lunatique Menu pips Bintcliffe. But first and third is Audi's best result for ages and there's much rejoicing over lunch of mixed grill in a bun.

But the weather's improving, which means it's getting worse as far as we're concerned. For race two, a decision is made to change the spring rates on both cars, a job which, with the aid of an air-driven spring/damper compressor, takes a tad over 20 minutes. In the tumult of ratcheting, banging and hissing of air, I fail to make any contribution whatsoever. Just as I reach out to pass a tool or spring, it disappears in a flash before my eyes, whisked away by sleight of practised hand, with the result that I just wobble around the car permanently half a second behind the proceedings. But I do manage to change some wheels, mop water from the cockpit and wax both cars again.

Then I put the fuel in. It comes in a huge plastic barrel with a sort of spring-loaded bung on the end. This is up-ended over a self-sealing filler in the A4's boot. Press down and the fuel just glugs in. Cock it up, though, and you'd fill your boots with petrol. A few blokes stand well within arms' length for this bit.

For the race, I'm elected to the board – Biela's pit board, that is. One bloke fills in the time and lap details from a huge box of letters and numbers, and I hold it out as he streaks past. I remember this race as a series of small numbers. Each lap, the man on the stopwatches turns with ashen face and yells in my colleague's ear. He then reaches into the numbers box, sometimes for a higher digit, sometimes a lower one. In my clammy-handed excitement I almost drop the board over the wall. It has happened, apparently.

But the track is just a bit too dry for the A4s. At the end it's Menu from Harvey, with Biela third and Bintcliffe fourth. But this is still excellent going, and the motorhome is full of rejoicing over the day's results. Yet even as Biela climbs the rostrum, the technicians are already beginning the huge, tedious task of dismantling the garage and packing all the equipment into the trucks.

I don't envy these guys so much now. The racing is much more exciting from the inside, but beyond that there's hard graft and too many weekends away from home. For two days, though, I felt the satisfaction of one who has made a contribution, even if it was only a small blob of elbow grease, the sundry of the pit lane. If you watched the races on the telly, you may just have noticed a bloke in the pit lane wearing a regulation Audi paddock fleece but completely the wrong trousers, looking knackered yet apparently doing sod all. That was me, that was.

PART 4 – THE THRILL OF THE OPEN ROAD (AT LEAST UNTIL THE PHOTOGRAPHER WANTS TO STOP AND TAKE A PICTURE)

A CHEAP HOLIDAY IN SOMEONE ELSE'S CAMPER-VAN MISERY

It is said that an Englishman's home is his castle. Rubbish. Kings and lords live in castles, and I'm pretty sure they're never asked to put some shelves up or do a spot of Hoovering.

It's why so many chaps have sheds. A shed offers the solitude that poets, philosophers and other deep thinkers have always craved; an oasis of personal squalor that some ancient and immutable social law says should not be invaded by anyone else.

Trouble is, a shed first requires a garden, and that, eventually, will need weeding. A more elegant solution is what I would call a camper van but what is more correctly known these days as a motor caravan.

A camper van offers similar sanctuary but with a constantly changing vista; a rolling shed giving access to the greater garden that is England's countryside. That same sense of fetid insularity can be enjoyed bang in the middle of a national park, with the added advantage that no one is going to ask you to mow it.

This was the plan – to travel, snail-like, with a microcosm of home at my back and to stay, alone, in those places where I'd often wished I could if only there was a hotel, but which would actually be spoiled by the presence of one. If not the middle of nowhere, then at least well into its interior. Exmoor, then – a part of the world pretty much as Adam would have known it.

On my first morning in the van, I had to acknowledge that I had only half succeeded. From one steamed-up window I beheld an expanse of soft green pasture complete with low-lying dawn mist and whinnying pony. From the other, an uninterrupted view of Exford Post Office.

I pulled back the camper's sliding door and met the postman. There was nothing for me. 'That's a pretty rough breakfast,' he said.

'What is?' I asked, even as the stench of burning reached my nostrils because I'd left the price sticker on the bottom of my new camping kettle.

'Boddingtons,' he said, indicating the array of spent cans on the floor.

'Nah,' I assured him. 'That was last night's dinner.'

This wasn't entirely true. The main course had been a robust steak 'n' chips at the nearby and slightly riotous Exford White Horse Inn, after which I had intended to drive a few miles up a road notoriously haunted by a spectral horse-drawn hearse (the harbinger of an imminent death, apparently) and into an area of moorland reckoned to be stalked by a giant, sheep-mauling black cat. There I would erect the hinged concertina that was the camper's extending roof and settle down to commune with nature, especially as there was no lavatory installed.

But as I drove an Exmoor fog descended so that, by the time I located a grassy pitch some 10 miles away, I wasn't sure if it was a layby or the green of a golf course. I sank into a fitful sleep but awoke an hour later with a thumping head and freezing feet. I'd parked on a slope and was sleeping the wrong way round. Reversing the bed arrangement restored a certain amount of inner calm but by now the pea-souper was host to every demon that had ever dwelt within the minds of men. And I'd forgotten to fill the integral water tank. So I returned to the village green, where the camper's curtains admitted a little of the warm and comforting glow given off by the windows of the Crown Hotel.

Still, breakfast – taken out in the sticks – would be a belter, and it was. Bacon, eggs, sausage, kidneys, beans, mushrooms, black pudding, tomatoes and some local and healthy-looking wholemeal bread. Everything except the tea, and including a few areas of the upholstery, was fried.

It's amazing what you can forget to take with you on a camper van holiday. Much of it is obvious – bedding, pans, pants – but those little things that are crucial to the smooth running of a household, and are taken for granted at home, are easily overlooked. Brown sauce, for example, and a pan scrubber. A sprig of Exmoor bracken makes an effective substitute – for the pan scrubber.

Bloody hell, I'd only spent one night and cooked one meal in the van, and it already looked and smelled like a student bedsit, an illusion enhanced by jazzy seat fabrics suggesting that the place hadn't been decorated since the '70s.

I suppose I should take a moment to introduce my unflagging ally on this trip; the Celeste Motor Caravan, converted from a Volkswagen Caravelle mini-bus by an independent company called Bilbo's Design. It's incredibly well thought out, and comes with a rear seat that converts to a double bed, a smaller bed area for an infant inside the accordion roof, a compact cooker, a fridge, a sink with electric pump and drainage tank, and curtains all round. There are two tables, a swivelling front passenger seat and battery-powered mood lighting.

If you want full sanitation and servants' quarters, you have to move further up the range and buy a true motor home, with a bathroom and what have you, but that will be something much bigger. The compact Celeste is really designed for use on organised caravan sites with shower blocks, and can be hooked up to a permanent mains electricity supply. It's a metal tent, if you like, only much better – it's properly equipped, entirely waterproof and comes ready assembled.

It's also a lot better than a normal caravan. For the enthusiastic motorist, towing a caravan is pure misery. They are slow, cumbersome, wide enough to become wedged in several parts of the Exmoor landscape, they create all sorts of rearward visibility problems and generally have even more tasteless interior trim. The Celeste is as wieldy as a large estate car and its rear-view mirror shows exactly what's behind you. The duvet, usually.

The downside of the motor caravan is that if you're going to own just the one vehicle, then you are committed to taking your holiday accommodation with you on every journey, even to the supermarket. This is deeply ironic in an age when so many of them will deliver to the home.

The mini-bus on which the Celeste is based is in turn based on a humble builders' panel van but, independent artisans being a much fussier breed than they once were, vans are pretty good these days. The Celeste – daft name, but it's a caravan tradition – fairly bowls along, the oily throb of its gutsy 2.5-litre turbo diesel overlaid with the rumble of an errant beer can somewhere in the back. It's worth taking a bit of care over correct stowage in these things. There's a place for everything in the Celeste and on the largely straight A-road route between London and the West Country everything seemed to be in its place, in accordance with the old maxim. Once on the winding stuff, however, I became reacquainted with a few items of unfinished washing up from the breakfast. I also forgot to latch the door of the fridge and got egg all over the floor.

I felt a bit of a fraud after the earlier Exford incident so my determined plan for the second night was to spend the day exploring the area and eating ice cream before locating a remote spot with a sea view for the night. And so I simply roamed Exmoor, returning the vigorous waves of other motor caravaners (this had me confused – I thought I'd left the roof up or something) and marvelling as the wonder of creation unrolled before me in widescreen format. And all the while I knew that I could, at any time, simply park up, brew up and even nod off.

How I laughed as I sped past the vacancy signs on family hotels and the hordes of people crammed into small restaurants. I admit, though, that it was quite difficult to drive straight past the Ilfracombe Tandoori with only the ingredients for a fish-finger sandwich on board.

Eventually, I settled on a small plot overlooking Woody Bay, arriving just as the sun tensed for its final plunge into the sea and threw a last, defiant burst of liquid gold over everything. Even a bottle of vegetable oil looked beautiful when illuminated by its reflected glory.

I raised the roof, erected the table and prepared the seafood delicacy. It was nine o'clock, and the remainder of the evening would be spent in reading and quiet contemplation; solitude and blissful silence broken only by the occasional interjection from a sheep in the adjoining field.

That night, as I lay in the faintly fetid interior of my Celeste, I wondered what it was that made the motor caravan so appealing to someone who would regard normal caravaning as the most loathsome experience on earth, were that accolade not already reserved for anything to do with tents. Something certainly did.

At around £28,000 the Celeste represents an outlay roughly equivalent to nearly 300 days' worth of quality bed and breakfast for two, or about 10 years' holiday accommodation. That's one way of looking at it, and a way that makes it seem expensive.

But here's another. It's still a good deal cheaper than that second home in the country we all secretly yearn for. Yet, essentially, that is exactly what it is. Anywhere you like.

THE MOTOWN STORY

I never much liked motor shows. This one's no different save for a few details, such as that the silvery ticket in my hand cost $250. But that's all right because it's all for charity and anyway, someone else paid. The women are largely in little black numbers and the blokes are in what Americans insist on calling tuxedos. This is gala night, the last and most exclusive preview before the doors are thrown open to Joe Six-Pack.

Mounting pressure on the thorax suggests that *Car Magazine* snapper Steve did a rather overenthusiastic job of tying my bow tie, but at least I'm wearing the one piece of clothing actually specified in the bottom right-hand corner of the invitation. Elsewhere, this has been dispensed with in favour of an invariably jewelled collar stud. This is not about cars at all, it's about the great and good of the city putting in an appearance, preferably a memorable one. People gush and so does bubbly, but sadly into that vessel that is so inextricably linked with civic functions and rejoices in a suitably ominous oxymoron – the plastic glass. Later, these will be found abandoned on boot lids or trodden into the carpet, like the aftermath of the school disco. At least Mercedes-Benz has real American beer in real, cool glass, but even here someone overhears our conversation and says, 'You guys are from Australia, right?'

Mustn't be cynical, especially as I got in gratis; look at cars instead. But this only makes things worse. Just what are European car makers trying to say? Everywhere there is fatuous imagery of furry animals and trendy young people, probably dolphins too if you look hard enough. On the VW stand the fine and handsome Passat is sidelined in favour of the ridiculous new Beetle, adorned with flowers and the current Miss Michigan. She has fine teeth, but then it's illegal not to in the US. Tiresome car makers' bicycles are irritatingly evident and the Porsche stand is showing a weird film of microbes and sperm, all to do with great ideas evolving or something. If Henry Ford hadn't hijacked the word for use elsewhere I'd say it was bunk. Now the Chevrolet Silverado, an awesome V8-engined pile of extended-cab pick-up displayed with funny-hatted and denim-clad chap strumming country songs on his guitar – cheap fuel, big distances and American liberty are all implicit in its unashamed bulk. That's more like it.

But we're not here for the sanitised version of events proffered by a motor show, we're here to discover the truth about Detroit, the cradle of motoring civilisation and the city the car industry built for itself. And the truth is not to be found in the cosy, glitzy surrounds of the Cobo Center. The truth, as ever, is out there.

The batteries in Steve's camera begin to fade at minus 10, and so do I. Fingers and mechanisms seize and conversation becomes difficult owing to numbing of the face. Detroit in January really frosts my ass, and it's tempting to think the American auto industry made an early blunder in the choice of its location. Michigan is the only state in the US from which, looking south, you can see Canada. Eh? Florida would have made more sense, you guys.

There are good reasons for things working out the way they did. The region belonged to the Wyandot people until 1701, when the white man came. Actually, it was a Frenchman, Antoine de la Mothe, sieur de Cadillac, an army captain sent by the king to establish a trading post and stem British encroachment into the area. He reputedly landed at the spot now occupied by the Renaissance Center, the '70s-built five-tower complex recently bought by GM for conversion to its new world headquarters. Cadillac named his settlement Pontchartrain d'Etroit, source of its current name. Some two centuries later, one Henry Leland, an admirer of the pioneering spirit and a man prepared to push the boundaries of manufacturing possibility, named his car company after the explorer.

For over a hundred years the tiny settlement – population 1,650 in 1810 – was fought over by the British, the French and the Indians. But by the time it was admitted to the Union in 1847 steam navigation was well established and the Erie canal had been built, which slashed the Detroit–New York journey time by 90 per cent. Detroit became an important shipbuilding centre and, with the opening of the railway to Chicago in 1852, a suitable transfer point for grain and lumber from the American interior. To the old world this promised work and prosperity, and Detroit's legendary immigration began. Towards the close of the century the population was up to nearly 300,000, following the influx of Irish, Italians, Ukrainians and, most numerously, Poles. Detroit was now famous for iron, steel, steam engines and ships, and as a world centre for cast-iron stove manufacturing. The infrastructure that would be required by mass manufacturing was already in place and with it the necessary technical skills. Walter Chrysler, after all, worked on the railways. By now Detroit was pretty much gagging for the horseless carriage.

When it came in 1896, trundling into town under the command of its creators Charles B King and his mechanic accomplice Oliver E Barthol, it was just that. It is preserved in the Detroit Historical Museum and really is just an ox cart with an engine lashed in the back. But, unlike Benz's effort, it had a full complement of wheels and that engine was a sophisticated in-line four. Already the American car business was looking cocky. It seems to have been well received, too, but then this was a town that thrived on new technology.

Ransom E Olds was Detroit's first proper car maker. He would have been Newark's, but a chance meeting on a railway platform with a copper magnate named Smith persuaded him to set up in Detroit in return for financial backing. He built the first car factory in 1899. It burned down two years later, but his timekeeper James Brady rescued the prototype Curved Dash Olds from the flames. He went on to become the mayor of Detroit, as was only right, for the Olds became the world's first series production car, with 425 built in 1901. Suppliers sprang up to serve the endeavour and Detroit was go.

The Olds was not *mass*-produced, mind, though it undoubtedly threw the gauntlet down in front of Henry Ford, who set up shop proper in 1903. General Motors came in 1908, with William Durant's incredibly far-sighted vision that a holding company should be formed to draw together numerous smaller and vulnerable car makers. Chrysler was a latecomer when he went his own way in 1925, but had the sense to buy up the inventive Dodge brothers and secure a reputation for innovation.

Living and working in Detroit must have seemed fantastic. Prosperity and hope were bolstered by the progress of the car, production of which occupied a quarter of the city's populace by 1929, a population that had grown five-fold since 1904 to 1.6 million. In 1911 Ford began building his Model T in a way no one had tried before, and in 1913 he brought production to a halt for the day to photograph his entire workforce of 12,000 outside the Highland Park factory. Times must have been good, for this may just be the world's most expensive photograph. A pristine example of the T is on display in the museum and, unusually, you are allowed to sit in it. Of this ground-breaking car Steve notes: 'The lofty driving position is spoiled by pedals that are too close together, like the Lamborghini Diablo's, and poor weather proofing. The controls do not fall easily to hand.' None of this stopped Ford producing 15 million of them by 1927. In 1920 half the world's motor vehicles were Model Ts.

The lure of Detroit was immense. A photograph surviving from the century's first decade shows a Ukrainian family of four with a few small suitcases. They have just stepped from the train, drawn halfway round the world by the promise of a new, better life in the bosom of the motor industry. After the first war, black families of the southern states flocked north in their thousands for the same reasons. An alarmist telegram to Henry Ford in 1923 reads: 'We are advised that rumors are in circulation throughout the entire south that the Ford Motor Company is seeking labor.' But then, Ford had doubled his standard labour rate to create the five-dollar day. Today, African-Americans make up around three quarters of the city's population.

Great edifices trumpeting the success of the city, such as the original GM headquarters and the neighbouring Fisher building, rose omnipotently from the low-rise sprawl. The motor barons were the heroes of the day; a picture of the youthful Alfred P Sloan shows a dashing fellow wearing the expression of a man possessed. In 1934 Clyde Barrow stole a Ford V8 for bank robbing and felt compelled to write to Henry Ford: 'Even if my business doesn't seem strickly legal, it don't hurt anything to tell you what a fine car you got in the V8.'

Even the Depression could not knock Detroit off course. Labour unrest in 1936 and '37 caused the famous sit-in strikes at GM's factories by the newly formed Union of Automobile Workers of America, but this, too, is recorded positively in the history books as the most beneficial labour movement of the century. It certainly didn't prevent Detroit becoming 'the arsenal of democracy' during World War II. Thousands more streamed to the city to make, among other things, 92 per cent of the vehicles, 75 per cent of the aero engines and 56 per cent of the tanks used by the US forces. Tens of thousands were drafted to build the B24 Liberator alone, which at one point was taking to the air at the rate of one an hour.

All of this, of course, simply left Detroit better equipped with skill and plant to begin, post-war, a new era of car building. This was the indulgent age of affordable muscle cars and Harley Earl's tailfins, themselves inspired by the warplanes that Cadillac had helped build through its work on Allison aero engines.

To many, the following 30 years are the golden age of the American car. My favourite exhibit in the Henry Ford Museum – not a collection of old Fords, but the legacy of the old man's efforts to record the history of the American people through the things they made – is Chrysler's obscure 1964 turbine car. Commercially it was not a success, but stylistically it is a masterpiece, festooned with turbine imagery in such details as its vaned headlamp bezels and wheel centres and the nozzle-like design of its rear lamps. It is the work of an industry still rejoicing in itself. But though Detroit's car business may have been on a roll at the time, problems were surfacing in the city which it had created and which served it.

Three years after the turbine car, the tragedy of Detroit was burned on to the world's conscience. It's been there ever since.

As we wait at the lights on Woodward, a beat-up '70s Chevy Camaro pulls alongside, engine throbbing. Green comes suddenly on American traffic lights, and as it does the Chevy's rust-ravaged bootlid squats and, with a squeal of rubber and a whiff of burned oil, it lunges for the next junction, just up the road. All the lights are red. He does it every time.

This sort of behaviour is not without precedent. In the '50s, Detroit's streets were the amateur drag-racing centre of the world, where young men in modified V8-engined cars wowed the crowd, often with the clandestine help of GM engineers keen to test engine developments in the white heat of downtown competition.

After a while I'm tempted, and the Seville STS's Northstar V8 burbles encouragingly. As the light changes I slam the pedal down, the exhaust note hardens and, whooping deliriously, we touch 80mph on the short drag to the next red before bringing the whole pointless, gas-guzzling charade to an ABS-assisted halt. We've beaten him by about 0.25 seconds.

Childish? Certainly, and pretty unfair given the 20 years that separate the cars. But hardly dangerous. This is downtown Detroit on a Wednesday afternoon and the pavements are deserted. Given that this is the epicentre of the world motor industry, the roads, too, are suspiciously free of cars.

'Donut development', as the Americans call and spell it, is not a phenomenon unique to Detroit. Happens in England too, that people move out to the suburbs and the shops and services follow. What we call the inner city ends up poor, underfunded, problematic. But Detroit is something else.

Turning from the main road to a deathly silent side street, we find rows of magnificent turn-of-the-century houses where once the captains of industry and commerce dwelt, and elegant '30s apartment blocks. All are derelict, some burned out. It is the occasional intact house that looks incongruous here. An abandoned wind chime sounds eerily from some long-ruined garden. The destruction, once you look, is everywhere

– cinemas, shops, commercial premises. Even Hudson's department store in the town centre, remembered by every old person we spoke to as the hub of the city's good feeling, stands as a multi-storey testament to Detroit's decay. The new shop is in the suburbs too. 'They couldn't lease that place for one dollar,' says a scarred Vietnam veteran I met in its shadows, who, tragically, is living on the street.

Postwar affluence has something to do with it. The GI Bill gave returning soldiers cheap loans to build new houses, and they did it in the suburbs. The car industry was wealthy, and wealth migrates outward, too. The very product that made the city, the car, allowed people to commute from afar. The suburbs are thriving still. Drive north to the inappropriately named Birmingham and you find an attractive and prosperous town of its own. Drive – there's no bus – east to Grosse Pointe and see fabulous mansions. Edsel Ford built one of them.

But the summer of 1967 was the turning point. Legend has it the famous riot started in an after-hours drinking den near the old Tiger Stadium, with a slanging match between aggrieved blacks and the predominantly white police force. 'It was a feeling that kinda burst out,' says one who, returning to the city that evening, couldn't even get to his street. 'It was a hot, sticky day. The sort of day when you might want to riot.' Inevitably, the rioters ended up destroying their own neighbourhoods. By the end of it 43 were dead, Detroit's 'nicely integrated' social fabric had come unstuck and age-old racial tensions were unfettered. On the streets you can canvass opinions from people of all parties, but their views are predictable and not worth repeating.

Realtors cashed in, buying people out of their houses for a song and selling them new ones in the suburbs at a handsome price, what we would now call a 'distress purchase'. Eventually some people simply abandoned their homes. Crime moved in. A campaign poster reads GUNS, GANGS, DRUGS – HAD ENOUGH? Not, as I said, a unique scenario, but what might be called a worst-case one.

Even the factories have largely gone. GM's Hamtramck plant, where Cadillacs are made, is the only one that can claim to be in Detroit proper. Its longstanding Clarke Street factory was torn down a few years ago, an event that still causes heartache amongst the General's executives. Ford's Highland Park factory, where the T was made, is now just a storage depot.

We drive back up Woodward and eventually find Piquete Street. The General Linen and Uniform Service looks like the right building, and gaffer Tom invites us in. Standing amidst the damp and flaking paint of the deserted upper floor, you can just get a sense of the building as it was in the photograph behind Tom's desk downstairs – half-finished cars tightly packed, men swarming around them. This is the factory where Ford built his 'alphabet cars', the models A, B ... everything up to the S, after which things were changed utterly. The steel sliding door through which completed cars were loaded on to trains is long seized. Tom's stationery cupboard was once a walk-in safe; the bricked-up window behind his desk was where men lined up for the fat weekly pay packets that had brought them here. But beyond the current tenant's personal enthusiasm, there's nothing to tell you what this building once was.

Detroit, we are told, is getting better. The carjacking and mugging we were warned against in its wrecked streets did not actually materialise. Plans are under way to regenerate the streets; the original GM building will be donated to the city and turned to wholesome civic purposes. All good stuff. But what Detroit needs is a sense of posterity.

A CLOT ON THE LANDSCAPE

As a good general rule, anything that involves dressing up – joining the navy, working in McDonalds, being a High Court Judge – is to be avoided. Invited to join the Land Rover Defender Challenge, essentially a two-day marathon of rolling around in the dust somewhere in Andalucia, I was advised that I would need to bring my 'adventure clothing'.

I had a quick rummage through the wardrobe and was relieved to find that I didn't have any, save for an old pair of Land Rover boots stolen during a factory visit.

'I haven't got any adventure clothing,' I said, 'so I won't be able to come.'

'Oh, don't worry,' said the PR lady. 'Just bring something old, so it won't matter if it gets ruined.' This immediately opened up the entire May spring/summer collection. 'Anyway, we can lend you something.' Bugger.

Several things distinguish Land Rover from other manufacturers. One is a steadfast refusal to use the word 'car'. A Land Rover is always a 'vehicle' and any sort of off-road activity is an 'expedition'. The other is the company's range of corporate clothing. Since Land Rover is all about conquering Africa and places like that, it's only reasonable that they should offer a comprehensive range of pith helmets, khaki shirts, safari jackets and trousers on which the legs unzip to create instant shorts. This is just what you need out in Kenya, surrounded by crocs and armed with nothing more than the cocktail stick from your last gin and tonic – selectable low- and high-ratio legwear. For the full comedy effect, remove just one leg.

And so it was that on the first day of the Defender Challenge I was standing by my vehicle and standing by to stand by in nicked boots, an old T-shirt that I thought looked very Land Rovery (because it's green) and adventure trousers. Meanwhile, the Land Rover staff emerged at the double in line astern looking like a platoon of the Queen's Own Off-Roaders, all crisp shirts, pressed shorts and proper haircuts and under the command of Sergeant-Major Roger Crathorne, Land Rover's head of off-road driving and all things decent, military and highly polished. 'This is a challenge,' he announced. 'You will get dirty, and you will get wet. Familiarise yourself with the vehicle.'

Essentially what you see here is a Defender 90 TD5 turbo-diesel, reputedly the world's most capable off-roader. It is obviously – pauses to light pipe and don woolly hat – a *proper Land Rover.* The body styling looks as if it was worked out in cardboard rather than Cad-Cam. It is a direct spiritual descendant of the Wilkes brothers' original knockabout farm utility vehicle of 1948 and in some ways hasn't progressed at all. All the door hinges are still on the outside.

But you have to wonder how much longer Land Rover will be able to call it the 90. As the figure refers to the wheelbase in inches, there's a good chance the Solihull Trading Standards Officer will confiscate the lot under some EU directive on SI units. It will then have to be rebadged as the Defender 2,286mm, and that will be England gone.

My Defender was offered in 'Expedition Spec', which means more auxiliary lights than I managed to count, various bash-plates and side steps, a powered winch mounted in the front bumper, a high-level engine breather for 'deep water fording' and aluminium tread plates around the bonnet that would allow me to 'climb up on to the wings'. Why? Sand channels and jerry cans were affixed to a sort of roof-mounted viewing platform reached by a ladder up the back, on which I would be able to stand and salute to the bitter end as I went down with my vehicle. It looked terrific. Where other off-roaders make some sort of 'lifestyle statement', this one is used by the army. The Defender 90 TD5 Expedition Spec is laden with kit and the promise of great suffering.

In the back were more things that should have been outlawed by the Geneva Convention – a selection of tow ropes, a shovel and a large axe with which I would be able to hack off my own arm before eating it. In the cabin, though, things were more promising. There was a radio, for a start, and a survival pack including choc bars, packets of tissues and bottles of mineral water. This was most encouraging, as by this point I imagined that getting a drink would involve straining swamp water through my pants or something.

The Defender Challenge began on the evening of my arrival, just at the point when I was ready for a beer and bed, with a night-driving exercise. Off-roading at night is something I'd never done before and it's quite interesting. I may have had the candle-power of a searchlight battery at my disposal, but even that would only illuminate a limited area of the Andalucian outback, especially when stuck halfway up a steep slope with all the auxiliary lights pointing at Venus. Twenty paces from the Land Rover there could have been almost anything – a proper road, perhaps – but your imagination conjures up something much more sinister. I reached through the window and swivelled the roof-mounted searchlight to check for hordes of spear-wielding natives and was startled when the beam briefly picked out a wild Brummie leaping through the undergrowth and emitting its characteristic cry of 'diff lock!'.

So far, the biggest dangers were being flayed by an unseen branch through the open window and attracting extra spud-peeling duties from the sarge for breaches of off-road etiquette. I retired to bed and spent a sleepless night, unable to breathe properly through all the crusty bogies that the dust had formed in my nose. I knew the next day would be worse because there had been some worrying talk of 'team spirit' over dinner.

It began easily enough with some rutted tracks, talk of axle articulation and more radio-relayed bollockings about the diff lock. Then we came to a river. 'In you go,' said Roger. 'Gently does it.' I removed the lower portion of my adventure trousers.

At first the Defender chugged indomitably through the shallows, generating a pleasing bow-wave in accordance with correct wading technique. Then the river deepened and a curious bubbling sound could be heard from the now submerged exhaust pipe. Then I noticed the rapid ingress of silty water through the bottom of the driver's door. This in itself was not actually a problem, as the Defender is waterproof right up to its steering wheel, but I found myself driving one-handed, the other engaged in a constant battle to keep mobile phone, tape recorder, walkie-talkie and the discarded parts of my trousers above the rapidly rising water line. I could no longer see my boots and my tuck box bobbed around in the passenger footwell, yet the Defender maintained steady progress.

But the river was deepening all the time. Soon the gear stick simply jutted out from a sea of brown like a dead branch. The wheels scrabbled for grip in the muddy riverbed, digging even deeper holes for the vehicle, and I had to acknowledge that my Defender had now arrived at that situation described in off-road parlance as 'sinking'.

'Leave me,' I ordered. 'Go on, and save yourselves.' It seemed sensible to sit tight, listen to España FM, eat my chocolate and hope for rescue by a craft better suited to the terrain. A boat, perhaps. As I settled down for the long wait I began recording some observations concerning the interior, or what I could still see of it. It's rather basic and free of any extraneous feature save the radio. It may now be largely devoid of bare metal but that essential hose-down quality survives in the slightly brittle plastics, and the Defender was to become the only vehicle I've ever jet-washed on the inside.

A man appeared on the bank with a stout rope. 'Out you get,' he yelled. For some reason that I still don't understand I clambered out through the window. Perhaps I sensed, instinctively, that opening the door would let water into the vehicle.

Up to my nads in the river, I attached a tow rope. But the ignominy didn't end with being hauled out. Though successfully beached, I noticed that the Defender was still full of water. A helpful colleague opened the passenger door to let it out, with the result that my rations were immediately swept overboard and back into the river, necessitating a second bout of wading to effect the most important recovery operation of the day.

I still wasn't in the clear, because there was a steep and seemingly unassailable bank to ascend. Incredibly, the Defender went straight up it, but when I returned to the slope to embrace the team spirit and help my stranded colleagues, I fell straight on my arse. This means either that the Defender is even more capable than I first imagined, or that more of the R&D budget needs to be spent in the boot department.

I wish it to be known that *Autocar* magazine made it up the bank thanks mainly to sterling spade work by your own correspondent.

Further along the trail was Land Rover's favourite off-road obstacle, the v-shaped gully. This is best approached at an angle, to prevent grounding out. 'Nice and steady,' said Sarge. 'This one could easily tip you on to the roof.' I put the nearside front wheel into the ditch and the Defender responded with a lightning blow to the side of the head with the door frame. An absurd angle of incidence was achieved, wheels hung in the air (diff lock!) and all unsecured objects in the cabin formed a neat pile on the passenger door. This was ridiculous. If I was going to end up on the roof I wanted it to be the result of a 150mph get-off in a mid-engined supercar, not of creeping forward at 0.2mph while surrounded by men from the West Midlands telling me how to drive.

But I have to say that I made it. The Defender may handle like a Bechstein on a real road but out in the cuds it will cross terrain that I'd hesitate to tackle on a donkey. As its chassis components are made largely of pig-iron it's virtually impossible to break, and if the bodywork sustains a few dents it somehow looks better for it. At the very least you could always just pull the thing apart and knock them out with the heel of your coarse boot.

I did slightly less well at the long and terrifyingly steep descent, followed by the dried-up watercourse and the equally long ascent up the other side, another standard off-road scenario that has the Land Rover squaddies rubbing their hands in anticipation of your failure.

Low range, first gear, diff lock, feet right off the pedals, thumbs outside the steering wheel in case an unseen rock sends it spinning wildly; down I went, *gently gently gently gently*, the engine moaning, the seatbelt threatening to take my head off, trickles of water re-emerging from under the seat and re-entering my boots.

The thud of the front wheels into the ditch, and renewed contact between the head and something of military issue hardness, was the cue to snick it into second and gun the diesel for the long and slippery climb. My one criticism of the TD5 blown diesel is that it can leave you a bit bogged down in the lower end of the rev range, and it's a bit of a double bummer to find yourself bogged down by both turbocharger technology and the terrain. The gearchange also owes a certain amount to Victorian railway engineering.

But at least I remembered to put the diff lock on. In fact, I had almost achieved a faultless performance and attained the summit when Roger came on the radio and said, 'That was very good,' which I somehow misunderstood as an instruction to drive straight into a tree.

In all I hit two trees, got stuck three times, forded two rivers, had two tows, made one dent in the Defender and lost one leg, but only off my adventure trousers. The total distance covered was only about 45 miles, but at least half of it was the really difficult stuff you see in the Camel Trophy brochure. Normally, the Defender would not figure highly in any discussion of vehicle refinement, but when I finally turned on to real tarmac again I felt as if I'd stepped on to a sheepskin rug after a day of walking barefoot through gravel.

Here is why I would, in the end, recommend something like the Defender Challenge. Off-roading around your local disused quarry is right up there with ironing your socks, but a proper 'expedition' with a genuine objective – a decent dinner and the beer I was hoping for on arrival – is, I almost hesitate to admit, pretty invigorating stuff. Best of all, and as with being flogged, you'll feel much better for it afterwards. Mainly because it's over.

DON'T FORGET YOUR TOOLKIT

My friend Sophie was on the phone, speaking in a slightly manic tone disturbing in most people but quite becoming in one who is half Italian. 'My aunt's given me her old car. Will you come with me to pick it up and drive it back?' Can't you do it by yourself? Where is it? 'In a little village on Lake Como.' Italy? *Fantastico!* That's altogether different. I'd be delighted. What is it, by the way? 'A 1967 Fiat Cinquecento.' Ah . . .

Lake Como is an unutterably beautiful place; much prettier, to my eye, than the slightly flashy neighbouring Lugano. The tiny village of Rezzonico, home to the previous two generations of the Langella family, is a haphazard pile of old houses crowding the water's edge as if drawing sustenance from it and growing there. Focal point of the community is the diminutive and ancient Capella de Sant' Antonio, patron saint of, er, things that have gone missing, apparently.

I press for explanation over dinner, a homely affair of local produce, gargantuan portions and several courses, the complete consumption of any one of which is taken to indicate unsatedness and generates a refill. If something goes missing, say the car key, then Nonna (grandma) says a quick prayer to St Antony and, like as not, it will turn up.

And if it doesn't? Doesn't this shake one's faith in the great martyr somewhat? 'Oh, no,' comes the translation. 'In that case it was actually *lost*.' By this point we were on course four, the freshly picked cherries. Bloated, I discreetly slipped handfuls back into the central bowl when no one was looking, and was thought to have acquitted myself admirably, portion-wise. Time to move on to the cake then. *Surely not*. Out came a huge slab locally baked in honour of . . . guess who? No, not me – St Antony. Anything not consumed there and then would be coming with us in the car. That Tony also moonlights as a guardian of travellers offered some reassurance. Presumably he would stop us from actually getting lost.

The omnipresence of the great saint was a glaring portent that escaped me in the excitement generated by the unveiling of the car that would be our trusty companion for the next five days. Bought new (locally, of course) in 1967 and promised to Sophie when she was a small child, the Cinquecento was a monument to the sort of originality that old car collectors covet. Every last piece of paperwork ever generated by this car, even old tax discs, survives in ordered, rubber-band-bound form. It came with the optional radio, but that hadn't been unpacked from its box yet; I even came across a letter from the salesman expressing hope that the car would prove satisfactory. Last year, the same bloke sold Sophie's aunt a new Cinquecento after a protracted example of what dealers call a repeat sales prospect. In the intervening 27 years the old car had never left Rezzonico and its environs. This, and the presence of St Antony on the metal dashboard in magnetic map-holding form, should have told me something.

For the first bit of the road to Lugano we were tailed by the relatives in the new car, they being fearful that the prospect of such an epic journey would somehow affect the '67 machine. I have never understood this thinking. Cars aren't human – it didn't *know* it was going all the way to England. It had covered about 35,000 parochial miles without a hitch; another 1,500, even in one go, wouldn't matter.

After 10 miles or so the chase car peeled away with a cheeky, Cinquecento-sized parp and we were alone on a superbly snaking road. Sophie drove, leaving me free to marvel at how the Italians could make such sense out of a concept as essentially barmy as the 500. This was studied simplicity – one tiny instrument and a few unmarked switches, pedals like French-horn keys and a lever in the back to redirect engine bay heat to the cockpit if desired. Brilliant and infinitely repairable – it's rumoured that Italian sweet shops keep a few essential Cinquecento spares. The whole, even from outside, exuded the musty smell of antiquity that identifies old cars – which I had also noticed, ominously, in St Antony's place back in the village. Uphill the engine throbbed, downhill it spun deliriously in true Fiat tradition. We discovered that despite its mere 500cc the Fiat could be made to bowl along, provided momentum was maintained, to the extent that we caught, and became frustrated by, a BMW 5-series being driven by worried of Munich.

Within an hour we had entered Switzerland and joined the motorway. Now the air-cooled two-pot fairly roared with endeavour and 80kmh was observed on the tiny, yellowing speedo. Eventually, in high spirits, we gained on a huge truck. 'Shall I overtake?' said Sophie, barely able to contain her excitement. Yes!

We crept past – I remember waving to the driver and him making a scooping gesture with his hand as if to help us along. We pulled back into the inside lane and then our whoops of delight were cut off like a snapped cassette by a loud pop accompanied by that horrible, hot smell so familiar to owners of old cars. Power tailed off dramatically: I made a quick appeal to the magnetic St Antony but no, all power was definitely lost. We drifted on to the hard shoulder in loaded silence.

No problem, though. There had been a noise, a smell and the generator light had come on. The fan belt had broken and starved the ignition circuit of current. Obvious. I'd worked this out before we even came to a halt, and of course we had brought a spare belt. I hopped out, flipped open the boot and, you may not be surprised to learn, the fan belt mocked me in its intactness. Through a pall of smoke I could see that oil was just about everywhere, except, I reasoned, in the engine. Even on the rear screen. It was at this moment that the image of my tool box, still sitting incongruously on my dining room table back in Blighty, sprang to mind.

As I walked back from the SOS telephone I suffered one of those sudden and depressing onsets of reality. What had I been thinking of when I agreed to 1,500 miles in an ancient Fiat 500? I keep getting involved with old cars, they always break and somehow I'm always surprised. We had covered but 38 miles and the car was comprehensively knackered. Even our (original) warning triangle was busted, and I soon tired of trudging the regulation 100 metres back to stand it up again. When the police arrived an hour later, they ran over it, and it now forms one of the random piles of crazed translucent plastic that grace all motorways. The police wandered around the car, rang a recovery truck, posed for a picture, fined us for not having a Swiss motorway pass and buggered off.

Two hours later we were towed to a Fiat garage in Bellinzona, expense mecca of the universe. A mechanic poked around the engine bay whilst discussing the problem with Sophie in the usual rapid-fire and unhinged-sounding Italian. She turned to me with an ashen face. 'The tree of the engine is broken,' she translated. I knew it.

The next day, sitting idly in a Swiss bar awaiting news of our repatriation, the true folly of our venture struck me. We had taken every precaution for its emigration: we had detailed maps and a carefully planned route; the car had been serviced and overhauled; we had the most comprehensive AA cover going and we had taken essential spares. Yes, I had forgotten the toolkit, but that was as irrelevant as all our other expedients. For as I bit into another piece of that cake to avoid paying £5 for a sandwich, I realised that I hadn't cleared the trip with the great Saint.

Broken tree my arse. This was a clear case of divine intervention. This car had returned to its space in the shadow of Antony's tiny chapel every day for the last 27 years. When we drove out of Rezzonico it went missing; as we crossed the border into Switzerland it was clearly about to become lost. And as Sophie had put her foot down, so had he. I had tested the patience of a saint and suffered for it.

Sophie Langella's Cinquecento has since been brought to England by the AA. She now lives happily with the car in Teddington, Middlesex. Following the breakdown, James May returned to Italy and joined the Monastery of St Antony, Padua, where he is said to live a life of repentance. He was prevented by a vow of silence from talking to us.

HARLEY-DAVIDSON, A HANGING OFFENCE

It's not often we have a hanging in *Top Gear*, so I'm pleased to be able to present one here, for the entertainment of the crowd.

In 1816, long before the motorbike was invented, a man called Isaac Harley was strung up at Ely, along with four other miscreants, for his part in the famous Littleport Riots. They'd only been protesting about the price of bread, for Pete's sake. It's not as if they killed anyone, although one Mr Speechley is said to have died later from the shock of the mob smashing his furniture up. They would probably have butchered a farmer called Martin had they been able to find him, but as they couldn't they settled instead for waving a meat cleaver over his aged grandmother's head. This and a few other minor misdemeanours were sufficient to condemn them to the drop.

From the newly erected gallows near the Ely workhouse, on Friday, 28 June 1816, rioter John Dennis confessed his crimes and implored the assembled people to 'avoid drunkenness, Sabbath-breaking, whoremongery and bad company'. Isaac Harley stated only that he met the death he had expected. Then they were despatched.

Good. It's the only language these people understand.

I hope you enjoyed the hanging as much as I did. Unfortunately, it may not actually be relevant to the story. It all depends on what else is unearthed by the Littleport Society, resident and highly active in the Fenland village of the same name. I wouldn't want to get on the wrong side of local historians. They know exactly what everyone's been up to for the past 500 years and might avenge themselves by tracing my ancestry and uncovering someone who was hanged. So we'll come back to Isaac the rioter later.

For now, let us move forward 19 years to 1835, when another Harley, William, was born on Victoria Street on the outskirts of the ancient village. The house is no longer in existence – and probably wasn't much more than a hovel, anyway – but Bruce Frost, treasurer, membership secretary and 'family tree surgeon' of the society, knows roughly where it would have stood. He pauses in silent awe for a moment at the spot that links this quiet rural road with what I thought was an all-American legend.

You see, in 1860 William Harley emigrated to America, where, as well as fighting in the Civil War on the side of the Union, he fathered several children with Mary Smith. One of these, William Sylvester, born in 1880, was the co-founder of Harley-Davidson in 1903 and the engineering brains behind its motorcycles. So there you have it. *Top Gear*'s Harley-Davidson Dyna Super Glide Sport is not, after all, the product of the great American dream; it is the product of Fenland seed, a commodity that was hitherto thought to yield nothing more than turnips.

I didn't know any of this. Neither did anyone else until 1996, when the Littleport Society revealed the connection. So when the editor of *Top Gear* said, 'We want you to take the long-term Harley home,' I envisaged the endless expanse and warm sunshine of Wisconsin, USA. Thanks to the pesky meddling Bruce

Frost and his Merrie Men, I got the vast expanse and leaden skies of East Anglia instead.

We've had the Harley for a year. *Top Gear*'s Road-test bloke Tom Stewart has been using it on and off for commuting and has pronounced it perfectly usable around town, which is quite a compliment when you consider that he normally rides one of those annoying little scooters. The magazine's 'art' bloke Marcel rode it to a Superbikes race meeting but ended up feeling a bit of a chump. I'd never been for a proper cruise on it.

'You may find,' said Tom Stewart as he handed me the Harley's keys, 'that you actually end up liking it. I did.' But he forgot to remind me that the Glide's ignition works independently of its steering lock. I therefore inserted the key under the seat, fired up the 88 cubic inch (1,449cc) beast, rode around in a small circle in the *Top Gear* garage, stopped, turned off, removed the key, unlocked the steering, reinserted the key under the seat, restarted the engine and finally headed out for Littleport.

I'd also forgotten that our bike has the optional Screaming Jessie ... sorry, *Screamin' Eagle* exhaust pipes. When I pressed the starter, I thought one of the cylinder heads had blown off. The first firing stroke sounds like a pistol discharging next to your ear, after which the 60-degree V settles down to a more general exchange of small-arms fire and road drilling. For a few seconds after starting, a warning light proclaiming 'engine' illuminates on the speedo. It should really be prefixed with 'Don't worry, that's only the'.

The racket is, in my view, embarrassing and deeply anti-social, but I seem to be alone in thinking this.

Everyone else in the *TG* office likes the noise, and even Bruce Frost, a non-rider but an admirer of Harleys, says, 'The noise is all part of the fun.' This is a strange attitude to adopt in a village that takes such a notoriously dim view of public disturbances.

In any case, the character of the Milwaukee lump is best appreciated through the arse, not the ears. The firing pulses are mercifully subdued through the bars and pegs, but through the seat of one's cowboy trousers an enjoyable relationship can be built up with the lazy torque characteristics, and one that renders the tachometer about as useful as the proverbial ashtray on a motorbike. The low-rev throb also seems to have a curative effect on minor aches and general early morning stiffness.

Then again, after an hour on the M11 I was convinced that I could wave goodbye to that other form of early morning stiffness as well, thanks to the sterilising frequency of the V-twin vibe. The Harley is not at its best on a motorway. The assault from the wind on the rider's partly reclined body is exhausting and the front wheel is prone to weave around a bit. On the back roads to Littleport, on the other hand, it felt remarkably at home, which only helps reinforce the idea that Harley-Davidson is imbued with Fenland breeding. A 50–60mph bimble suits its riding position and temperament much better, and I can see what editor Blick meant when he said, 'It's good at doing what it does best.' East Anglia, being flat and sparsely populated, even looks a bit like my perception of the great American outdoors.

Except that there are bends in the fens, they can conceal agricultural machinery, and the Harley has the worst brakes I've experienced on a road-going vehicle since I last drove a traction engine, which had brake blocks made of poplar wood. And this 'Sport' version of the Dyna Super Glide has *two* front discs where most Harleys have just the one.

Poor brakes are simply inexcusable on a new motorcycle. Barely more palatable are the price (£10,495), the lacklustre performance and the shocking detail finish. For a 3,000-mile bike that spends much of its life garaged, our Harley is looking pretty scruffy. There is chrome peeling off the rear spring hangers, the forks and wheels are flaking, the plastic trim is coming off the tank and the engine cases are adorned, like many of the bike's owners, with unacceptably furry nuts. I can see the theoretical appeal of a Harley – easy riding, low stress, a quirky nature – but by the time I arrived at the offices of the Littleport Society I was merely bored and irritated by it. I was also bent double by the whole experience and would have welcomed being hanged by the neck for a bit, though only until straightened out.

Which reminds me. The provenance of Harley the bike builder is beyond doubt. But what of Isaac Harley the rioter? Is he by any chance related? Bruce Frost hopes so. The year 2003 will be the centenary of Harley-Davidson, and the people of Littleport like to think that the company will want to conduct some celebrations in this, its spiritual home. If they do, Bruce has a slogan ready: 'Littleport – from rioting to riotous riding'. All he has to do is establish a connection.

Extensive lurking in graveyards and poring over parish records has revealed this much. There were two

Harleys, Jobe and another Isaac, living in Littleport in the 1700s. William, the father of the co-founder, has been traced back to Jobe; Isaac the rioter has been traced back to the earlier Isaac. 'I have the family tree with me if you want to see it,' says Bruce. I quickly stop him. It's about six feet long and compiled in a typesize more normally associated with insurance cover notes.

But if these two elder Harleys can be shown to be brothers, then bingo, Bruce's Harley jigsaw is complete. He is visibly excited at the prospect.

Then again, if several thousand Hog enthusiasts descend on this sleepy village with their Screamin' Eagle pipes and leather chaps, he may regret that he ever dabbled in this local history lark. He may even wish he could invoke the powers of those special constables appointed after the riots to ward against 'parties standing idly in the streets of the parish of Littleport'.

He may even end up thinking, as I am inclined to, that they hanged the wrong Harley.

I'M JUST GOING TO ICELAND, I MAY BE SOME TIME

From about 2,000 feet I could see, from the window of the aeroplane, that the landscape was pretty uninviting. Frosted, treeless, volcanic, desolate and rising only vaguely from the heaving grey bosom of the North Atlantic. I had my penknife and my compass; my adventure hat and my stout boots; my spectacles, testicles, wallet and watch. But, I suddenly realised, I'd forgotten my coat.

Maybe this wasn't surprising. If things had gone according to the original plan, I'd have written this on the sun-drenched terrace of a posh hotel in Johannesburg, with a flunky standing by ready to bring me another gin and tonic.

As it happens, this is a Land Rover drive story, and experience should have told me that anything less than an untimely death miles from civilisation would be a fair result. Let's have a look at the scoreboard to date: I nearly drowned in a Land Rover on the Defender Challenge, I got lost in a desert in one and thought I'd have to eat the photographer, I once left home in a Land Rover only to return on foot 12 hours later, leaving the thing teetering on top of a huge boulder somewhere, and I successfully drove a Discovery all the way to the northern tip of Alaska only to then lose it in a snowdrift.

Despite all this, I've become something of a fan of the Land Rover 'expedition'. So when Richard Newton and I were given the opportunity to drive the new Range Rover 12 weeks in advance of its launch, along with permission to go 'anywhere within reason', it seemed like a good scheme to spend four whole weeks driving all the way from London to the heart of South Africa. A couple of events served to quash this idea. Firstly, and quite by chance, I met a bloke in a pub who had made precisely the same journey in his own Land Rover, and it had taken him six months. Then another bloke called Bin Laden started a war, as if to reinforce my late grandmother's contention that you should never trust a man with a beard. It was thought that at some point on the trip the priceless prototype luxury off-roader might suffer a fate normally reserved for unattended packages at airports and be destroyed in a controlled explosion.

So I closed my eyes, Newton spun the globe and I stopped it with my fingertip. Risky, but I paid enough attention in double geog to know that the warm bits are round the middle. My intrepid index finger alighted on Pakistan. Most excellent. As a significant part of our old empire, it was the obvious place to put this triumph of Anglo/German engineering through its paces. And so, to cut to the chase, we went to Iceland.

We were, nevertheless, still mildly excited when we finally gained access to Reykjavik's container port to collect our sea-freighted vehicle. The customs docket proclaimed 'one piece Range Rover' but in fact we got the whole thing. This was the first time I'd seen it and I thought it looked pretty good; sort of still like the old Range Rover but not quite the same. I couldn't quite see what all the fuss over the headlights had been about, but that might have been because they, along with much of the rest of the car, were still plastered with the gaffer-tape disguise it had worn on the clandestine journey from Solihull to Grimsby docks.

I learned something curious about gaffer tape. In its normal role as the essential fabric of the May household it seems barely able to stick to itself. Yet at minus five or so it acquires great tenacity and a tensile strength slightly above that enjoyed by fingernails. Every hour or so a customs man dressed in Ernest Shackleton's own coat would emerge, watch for a few minutes and then retire to his geothermally heated office equipped with some interesting new Saxon words.

By the time we'd cleaned the car up it was pitch black. I looked at my watch and it was 4.30.

Besides the requirement for a decent coat, there are other factors to consider about Iceland in general and in winter in particular. What seems to be the world's most aptly named country could readily have been called something else.

Priceland, for example. There appears to be but one Indian family in Reykjavik and, joyously, they own a restaurant. Normally, foreign curry is a wishy-washy affair modified for timorous local palates and not like proper British curry at all, but this was pukka stuff: flavoursome, authentically spicy and altogether good enough to generate the phenomenon of a 'curry coat'. But then we got the bill, and it came to over £70. Even a pint was almost a fiver. No wonder hardly anyone lives there.

It could also reasonably be called Windland, since the fierce, icy breath of the Nordic gods could be unleashed suddenly and horribly upon the quaking, coatless carcass of your hapless correspondent at any time. Even Rainland would have sufficed for the day of our arrival, when the capital looked unnervingly like Manchester, but populated with fewer and more comprehensible people.

But personally, if I'd discovered the place in winter, I'd have gone for Darkland. Whereas the rest of us live through a year of alternate days and nights, Iceland effectively has just one of each and they're both very long. This may go some way to explaining why all the locals were a bit squiffy. In November the sun doesn't come up until gone 10 o'clock, and then only just, and five hours later it's gone again. If, like us, you can't afford to go to the pub, you end up back in the sack by nine.

It's a great excuse for not getting up early and it's a pity the traffic warden didn't see it that way. It's as well that a parking fine is one of the few things that could be considered good value in Iceland, with what would be a £40 or £50 ticket in London weighing in at just over a tenner. This seemed a trifling amount by local standards, so I threw it in the Reykjavik municipal bin. Bloody Vikings.

We needed a plan. A glance at the map showed that there is a road running all the way around the periphery of the island, Route One. There is no Route Two. From Route One various unmade roads, marked in brown on the map, lead off to what might be termed areas of outstanding natural beauty. We would complete a lap of the ring road, absorbing local culture as we went, and peel off occasionally to bring you pictures of the new Range Rover with a famous waterfall, geyser or whatever. This would give a thorough on- and off-road assessment and allow me to draw fatuous parallels between herring smoking and the workings of the transfer box. Job done.

And so we left Reykjavik. After about 500 yards we were stopped by a Land Rover enthusiast in a Defender fitted with balloon tyres that would refloat the *Titanic*. I outlined our itinerary and he looked at me as if I'd come outside without my coat on.

'These roads are closed,' he said, dismissing two thirds of the map with a sweeping gesture. 'These hotels are not open in winter' – that was most of the north and east. 'These are not the right tyres. You must drive in pairs. You need radio and you must tell police. You will need,' he said, tugging at a giant puffa jacket stuffed with albatrosses, 'proper clothing.' So these people inherited dour logic as well as hairy faces from the Scandinavian settlers of 1,200 years ago.

'We do not like it when the tourists die,' he said kindly. He had a point. Perhaps if I actually bothered to read *The Vehicle-Dependent Expedition Guide*, a gift from Land Rover and about as subtle as a deodorant at that, I would be a lot better at this sort of thing. Instead, I've resorted to things like DIY in a bid to put it off and remain, as a result, a complete off-road bonehead.

Still, as Magnus might say, we'd started, so we'd finish. If we could just reach the tip of the famous glacier at Myrdalsjökull in the south we could still feel pretty chuffed with ourselves. To begin with, though, we'd make a brief and exploratory foray to the Blue Lagoon geothermal power station and hot tub complex.

Occasional breaks in the all-enveloping fog revealed a landscape in which one wouldn't be entirely surprised to see a dinosaur. Volcanic activity has much to do with it. Iceland is something of a geological upstart at a mere 20,000,000 years old and is to the planet what an especially angry spot is to your nose. One day it, too, will erupt but in the meantime it provides limitless free energy. There's so much of it tapped at the lagoon that there is enough left to create a giant outdoor spa. It smells a bit eggy but it's hot enough to poach you while, absurdly, your exposed hair freezes into a single solid entity like the clip-on hair of one of those Lego people.

This is hardly intrepid stuff. Back aboard the Range Rover I located, amongst a lot of buttons that at first didn't seem to do anything, one that made the steering wheel heat up. This was most welcome, as it was a bit parky and I hadn't felt the benefit of my coat when I went outside after my bath, as my mother would say.

We drove through the troll-infested darkness towards Hvolsvöllui, from where certain operational patterns began to establish themselves. Firstly, the hotel was shut, but when we rang the number pinned to the door a man appeared, opened up a couple of rooms, muttered something from deep within the hood of a much-coveted snorkel parka and disappeared into the eternal night.

Secondly, words like Hvolsvöllui are virtually impossible to pronounce at all and especially in the correct rounded Icelandic manner. A Big John Hamburger eaten at a local roadside fuel stop was a *Big John Hamborgarar*, and if you wanted it with an egg it was *og egg* and cost £18. Liquorice Allsorts were *Apollo Lakkris*, coffee was *kaffi* and milk was *mjólk*.

It's not a real language at all, it's just a sing-song version of our own brought on by too much *Viking Bjor*.

Thirdly, the weather was always crap. The next day, earmarked for our first attempt at the glacier, was foggy and rainy again. If we reached our objective I wouldn't be able to see it and wouldn't be able to say, 'The vast plateau of the Myrdalsjökull glacier might have served as a model for the torque curve of the excellent BMW-derived V8,' so instead we visited the Skogar Folk Museum.

I recommend this. The curator, who is called something like Thor, is completely bonkers. Most of Iceland as we see it today is modern – its oldest hotel was built in 1930 – but Thor entertains us with evidence of earlier civilisations, including numerous artefacts wrought in desperation from the shrivelled genitalia of animals. I recall a short rope made from an ox penis and a money bag formed from a pig's scrotum. The first settlers, he explained, were Irish monks who built monasteries from 'turds and stones'. Then he sat at the harmonium and played 'O Susannah' and 'Rock of Ages' while forcing us to sing along in Icelandic. And then we ran away.

That night, in another abandoned hotel in a place called Vik, the wind roared again. The following morning the weather was even worse. This sort of thing went on for three days, the temperature gradually falling and snow and sleet joining the dizzying cycle of wind, rain, darkness, herring, Viking Bjor, empty hotel, bed. The postcards seen in Icelandic hotel receptions are less than honest. One popular example seen everywhere shows a brightly coloured puffin sitting atop a sunlit, moss-covered rock. The reality, as Newton's own picture records, is a rain-lashed clump of black volcanic debris with no puffin on it.

We had already covered some 750 miles around Route One in our attempts to snatch evocative pictures in rare bursts of late-afternoon watery sunshine. I was convinced of the Range Rover's luxury car credentials. The engine and gearbox are good and a suitable war reparation following the shenanigans over the owner-ship of Land Rover. The ride is simply outstanding for an off-roader and almost Jaguar-like at times. I'd worked out what everything on the dash did without recourse to the handbook, which in any case, this being a prototype, hadn't been printed yet. I could make it rise and squat on its magic suspension and Newton even managed to tune the telly in, though the picture was affected by what the TV repair man would call 'snow'. And so, with 24 hours remaining before the car had to be back at the docks, we finally made our bid for off-road glory and the tip of the glacier.

It started well. We scrabbled easily along the vague track leading north from Route One. We bounced over rocky mounds and forded streams; we selected low range, dived in and out of gullies and drove on for mile after breathtaking mile, a towering primaeval moun-tain vista to our right, a wilderness still awaiting the moment of creation on our left. This was more like it.

Everything seemed to go wrong at once. First we came to what looked as if it could be a frozen river, so I took the precaution of sending Newton ahead to probe the terrain with the extended leg of his camera tripod. One moment he was a six-foot specimen of fine European manhood striding forth into the unknown, the next he was a legless, flailing torso. Then the temperature dropped to minus 15, it went dark, and a distant mountain that had hitherto formed the backdrop to the scene was instantly obliterated by an approaching storm. So we turned and fled.

It was the right decision. By the time we reached our night's lodging in the tiny hamlet of Skálholt a good two feet of snow had fallen. The wind was so strong that it blew me over when I climbed from the car. The worst storm the locals had seen for three years raged all night and had intensified by the next morning, so that by 2.00 p.m. we were still stranded, 50 miles from the capital.

I lay on my bed and contemplated life, the new Range Rover and everything. I said that anything short of an untimely death miles from civilisation would be a fair result, so in that sense we had succeeded. At the same time, I was haunted by a mental image of the navigation lights of the once-weekly Grimsby-bound container ship receding across the bay in Reykjavik. Bugger. Once again, there were going to be some terribly disappointed people at Land Rover.

POLICE CAR, LIGHTS, ACTION

We're dealing with the sharp end of the law here, so for the usual legal reasons our 'victim''s name has to be concealed. I can tell you that he's in his mid-20s, and that even in the dimness of the Omega's rear seat his whole head looks a mess – dirt, bruises, old scars and vivid new stitches, the legacy of one of the roughest upbringings the country has to offer. The nature of our meeting suggests the *inside* of his head isn't in much better shape either, the legacy of a hard drug habit. 'A typical Glaswegian thug,' I am discreetly informed. We'll call him Bastard.

'Why'd you do it this time then, Bastard?' asks the driver, a hint of despair in his voice.

'I can't help it, man, I'm addicted to it.'

'You did it for the chase, yeah?'

'Aye. I'd love a smoke, you know.'

But smoking isn't allowed in police cars, and is impossible with your hands cuffed behind your back.

The atmosphere in the police Omega is relaxed, anticlimactic, friendly even. PC Kyle Morrison and Bastard are obviously well known to each other. Some of the 32 previous convictions have seen to that. They chat.

'That was the same route you took last time, you know,' says Morrison, incredulously, as we pull up at base and our fugitive climbs awkwardly out. Another officer discreetly holds a lit cigarette to his lips so he can have a few drags before being bundled inside for questioning. As he disappears, Bastard turns to me. 'You from a newspaper then?'

'*Car* magazine.'

His face lights up. 'Max Power, yeah?' And then he's gone. The dark car pound is near silent except for the lurch of cooling engines and the barking of Brodie the police dog from the back of the Volvo, and the air is heavy with the stink of roasted brakes and clutch plates. The bastard has just nicked another car.

Chief Inspector Alex Martin of the Strathclyde Police Traffic Group is well aware that police pursuit work is a controversial subject. Speed, as any traffic cop who has just stopped you will be quick to assert, kills.

'There's always been a car-crime problem in the north side of Glasgow especially,' he explains. The area he covers is host to some notorious housing estates, where car theft is just one branch of a lawlessness that involves serious drugs, burglary and violence. Traditionally, one third of all vehicle thefts in Strathclyde have been made in his area, and over a third of the force's car chases take place on the Chief Inspector's patch.

'If it became known that the police would never exceed the speed limit we'd never catch any of these bad guys,' he says – and these are guys who are often 'on the fringes of other criminal activity', guys who always make a run for it. 'But at the end of the day our people are ordinary drivers and subject to the same rules as everyone else, and should they be involved in an accident while driving a police vehicle, then that will be fully investigated. Should there be sufficient evidence, and I admit there are occasions when there has been, then they are reported for careless driving.

Our guys are not immune, and I believe that's only right.'

The Scottish approach to the issue, like some aspects of Scottish law, is slightly different from the English one but is still based around intensive driver training. It's obvious that Martin and his men regard the driving school at Scotland's Tulliallen Police College as quite simply the best in the world. But where some English traffic cops are taught specific pursuit driving skills, the Scots are not. The point is that police driving should not be a specialism, but rather just driving to a highly advanced standard. This is critical to Martin's safety argument. 'We believe there's no need to teach pursuit driving; if you can teach someone to drive safely at speed, that should be enough.'

The seriousness of Glasgow's car-crime problem led, in 1994, to the formation of Strathclyde's special Stolen Vehicle Squad, a collaboration between the traffic and dog departments and the outfit we are to join for a Monday night shift. The dog is a crucial but last-resort member of the team: in the event of a 'bale out' – when the thief abandons the car and legs it – then the dog can be called in to bring him down. One member of each shift is always a specialist dog-handler, a man who lives with the dog at home and work and will probably adopt it as a pet at the end of its working life. It can be hard on the dog – last year one was stabbed by a desperate fugitive.

Rivalling the dogs as stars of the SVS roadshow are two fully marked-up Volvo T5 estates. They are standard cars but for the usual police paraphernalia: a dog pen that fills half the load bay and extends into the nearside rear seat to allow a quick exit through the door, and uprated pads and discs sourced from 'a racing outfit'. The Volvos were chosen for reasons of acceleration, braking and handling that allow it to keep touch with a recklessly driven lesser car without taking risks at junctions, red lights and any other hazards at which a police driver *must* slow down.

The two Volvos usually work in conjunction with a fully equipped but unmarked car that can scout unobtrusively and then call in the marked cars if necessary. The T5s are famous among the locals. If absolutely necessary, a police helicopter can also be called into action.

The squad is successful. 'Car crime *is* going down,' says Martin. Last year the outfit made 348 arrests and recovered stolen vehicles worth half a million pounds. The shift starts at 19.00 hours.

The rear seat of a police car. A stiff-shirted, slightly intimidating figure up front, and the constant crackle of radio that is the leitmotif of law enforcement. I am in tonight's unmarked car, Rover 800 callsign Tango Mike Eight, with PC Malcolmson.

By 19.30 reports come through of a recklessly driven silver Honda, registration unknown but possibly stolen, on one of the Possil Park housing estates. The plain car's siren goes on and I am treated to the curious sound of a police car from the inside: strangely muffled, constant, without the doppler effect. We drive briskly through the town – 'making progress', the police would call it. I am forbidden by the terms of my being here to record the speeds reached, but in any case when I ask how fast we're going Malcolmson says 'thirty' without hesitation. He later also warns me to be careful what I say if we become involved in a pursuit – the standard in-car video is now equipped with sound recording, so that the mandatory police driver's commentary can supplement the video evidence in court. 'Very helpful to the jury,' says my driver; not so helpful if I'm screaming blue murder from the back seat. But the Honda has gone to ground.

Back at base we meet up with the two marked cars and Brodie, the German shepherd which, at a word from his master, PC Gordon Harper, would pin me against the wall. 'Otherwise he could go into a schoolyard full of kids and happily play around.' Good dog.

An hour's cruise around in Omega Tango Mike Six introduces me to the Ruchill estate, dilapidated epicentre of Glasgow's car crime and a place where law-breaking often begins in childhood. 'We stopped a car last week,' says PC Andy Pryde. 'The driver was 15, and there was a 14-year-old, two 13-year-olds and a 12-year-old on board too.' A burned-out Astra in a strip of waste ground stands like a portent; there is a soft tinkle of broken glass as a hurled bottle falls short of the car. The police have no friends here.

As I switch to the T5 at 21.15 another sighting of the renegade Honda comes through, lights and sirens go on and the Volvo bounces off its rev limiter as it screams to another area of Possil Park. I catch sight of a scrawled slogan on a derelict wall – 'fuck the polis'. I was warned that Brodie has a strange sixth sense for crime, and as we enter the estate he begins to bark madly. We find the abandoned Honda Civic, largely intact, but the steering column surround and ignition barrel are torn apart. 'Cars are still too easy to steal,' confirms PC Pryde. A gang of young lads hangs around 10 yards off, watching. The cops know one of them may well be the culprit, but no one's going to grass anybody up here.

Honda Civics are popular tonight. At 22.10 the radio jabbers out reports of a stolen dark-red one. Again we shriek to its last known location, a residential area about half a mile square. The drivers know the roads like cabbies; know that if they lurk at the two likely exits from the estate while the plain car goes in, they might catch the Honda as it bolts. If it's still in there. We sit with the windows open, listening for the squeal of tyres that is the signature of joyriding. Nothing. After over an hour we admit defeat and return to base for tea break.

At midnight, with the kettle not yet boiled, the hand-held radio delivers a cool, emotionless report that the Honda has been sighted on the run. The world goes mad, cups and chairs fly as the squad scrambles for its cars. I find myself back in the Omega, grappling with the rear seat belt – this is a police car – as insane acceleration and cornering toss me around the rear bench. The three cars split up and head for the last sighting at the Milton estate, hoping to outflank the 'target vehicle' on all sides.

The Rover spots it first. The radio explodes with instructions aimed at getting a marked car in pursuit, after which the Rover will back off but stay in touch – its job then is to video the action from behind in the hope of presenting the bigger picture. Within a minute the Volvo has latched on to the Honda's tail.

But we go the other way, drawing on detailed road knowledge to box the Honda in and contain the pursuit. Across a strip of rough ground I glimpse the lightless Civic pursued by the wailing T5. I see it again, going the other way, as we jockey for an intercepting position. The choreography, absurdly, is reminiscent of a Keystone Cops car chase but the mood is deadly earnest.

We make the interception, but the Honda is driven hard at us and PC Morrison backs off – a deliberate collision is not an option. We join the end of the flashing, bawling train and peel off again. I realise then that the Civic will never break away from the housing estate – it is a matter of time and careful manoeuvring, manoeuvring at speeds quicker than I can think or blurt my own commentary into my tape recorder. The swerving, bucking Honda is ever more contained, driven into decreasing circles of hopelessness. Crowds form on pavements and jeer at the police cars. Missiles are thrown. A brick strikes the windscreen of the Rover and destroys it; another does for a Volvo door skin.

An officer on foot appears as we move in from the flank again – I honestly couldn't tell you where or when he was dropped off by a fourth car – and deploys Stop Stick. This, an evolution of the notorious Stinger, is an extending, triangular-section aluminium strip with razor sharp edges, but shrink-wrapped in plastic for safe handling. It is flung across the road just as the Honda appears, and I actually see it drop as the tyres are savaged. In the split second before the pursuing

Volvo arrives at the same place it has been whipped away by a cord.

Now the Civic slews across an open expanse towards a corner bound in by raised pavements and iron bollards, the Volvo still glued to its tail. We move in on its open flank. It cannot escape. Yet still the driver won't give up, aiming for a gap between the metal posts and mounting the pavement with an audible clang from the Honda's nearly naked wheels. The Volvo cannot follow – insufficient ground clearance. But the Omega, with its higher ride height and sump guard specified as a result of painful experience, can. We pursue the now decrepit Civic until its suspension finally collapses. In the time it takes me to climb through the rear door PCs Morrison and Pryde have pinned the culprit to the ground and handcuffed him. Car thieves have been known to be armed.

Calm, professional detachment has immediately asserted itself. I'm reeling from the sheer terror of it all, but the aftermath of the chase is deeply sobering. Someone's Civic LSi is completely trashed, two police cars are damaged, cooked brake pads and discs will all be replaced as a matter of course. It seems a destructive and expensive way of collaring someone who, the police would say, should have been banged up long ago anyway.

But I'd be a liar if I didn't admit that the experience has given me a ghoulish thrill. The whole issue of joyriding and police pursuit is heavily clouded with political and sociological arguments, but in the end nicking cars is nicking cars. And I have to say we got the bastard.

THE SMART CAR. NOT AFTER WE'D FINISHED WITH IT.

There must be more important things in life than the colour of your car, but anyone who has ever owned a brown one will know that, somehow, it matters.

I've had 15 cars in my motoring lifetime and seven of them, including the current one, have been dark blue. A psychologist friend tells me this is a good thing. He points to something called the 'achievement motive', which says that dark colours are preferred by people who are going places. You might imagine that go-ahead types are roaring around in yellow sports cars, but a little study of any merchant bank's car park or the spaces reserved for our captains of industry reveals that the real movers and shakers of this world are tooling around in sober-hued executive expresses. Bright-red Ferraris and mint-green Porsche 911s are obviously for playboys, tarts and wasters.

So I'm quite pleased to have a dark-blue Jaguar but sometimes I look at it out of the window and wish it was orange.

This wouldn't be a problem if I had an MCC Smart, because for between £450 and £700 you can have all the Smart's plastic body panels changed for something completely different. There is an official Smart centre within half a mile of my house and the job takes about 30 minutes, or less time than some haircuts. I could drop the car off, have the rug rethink and arrive home a new person. The Smart is the only car that allows you to do this.

The *Top Gear* staff have a Smart + Passion Cabrio and, predictably, within a few months of taking delivery they were bored with it being all black. They thought it would be a good idea if I drove it all the way back to Smartville, the factory in Sarreguemines on the French/German border, to effect an identity crisis.

The blokes down the pub didn't, reasoning that a Smart was inappropriate for a 960-mile round trip. But this is missing the point. If the Smart isn't usable as a normal car, then it will actually contribute to the very problem that it purports to help solve – that of urban mobility and parkability. A pure city car is a pointless idea, as it will require every owner to have another, proper car for long journeys. That means that for every Smart prowling the streets of London, Manchester and Edinburgh there would be another, full-size car parked by the road somewhere, which amounts to one-and-a-half cars where previously there was only one. Bad result.

So with a fruity rasp from the 54bhp three-pot, that staunch mucker Lensman Debois and I headed for the far side of France laden with 1,001 pieces of camera equipment and one spare pair of pants for me. On paper the *Top Gear* Smart is a mid-engined, rear-wheel-drive, two-seater convertible Mercedes, but this won't quite wash with your mates, nor does it quite stack up on the A26 out of Calais, where the car's top speed of around 84mph is pretty much smack on the French autoroute speed limit. A long incline leaves it slightly winded and turning on the air con is like giving it a swift punch in the guts.

I have one or two other minor criticisms. The tachometer, mounted in a sort of robot's eyeball thing on top of the dash, can be swivelled away from your line of sight. Why? So your passenger can keep an eye on the revs for you? And why must cheeky little cars always have cheeky little horns? The Smart's hooter sounds like the battery-operated Pifco item I had on my childhood bicycle and for some reason seems to be directed into the cabin rather than outwards from underneath where the bonnet would be if the Smart had one. *Toot-toot!* Hello, said Noddy.

Otherwise, driving the Smart on a long journey is a bit like driving a car. The seating position is good, the radio works and the mechanicals thrum away fairly unobtrusively. It's surprisingly comfortable. In fact, from the driving seat it is easy to forget that the Smart is such a small car, because the view forward is like that out of a mid-size MPV.

But then, the Smart isn't really a small car at all, just a very short one. The original Mini or Cinquecento is a truly small car: a proper four-seat car built to a slightly smaller scale than a normal one. The Smart is to the same scale as an A-class Merc; it's just that, like so many things in life, it comes to a rather abrupt end.

Shortness has its advantages – it's obviously good for parallel parking – but a few busy French towns reveal that shortness counts for Jacques Sheet in terms of traffic-busting capability. In a traffic jam, the eight-foot, two-and-a-half-inch Smart has to wait in line just as the 17-foot Bentley does, because the length of the road is not the issue. To beat congestion you need to be narrow, which is why couriers ride motorcycles.

But it does get there. After 10 hours of autoroute, routes nationales, evil coffees and restorative games of bébéfoot, we arrived at Smartville. It's a large and very modern complex shaped like a giant plus sign and clad in white tiles, which can presumably be changed for red ones if they get fed up with it. Completed and brightly painted Smarts spill out of the end of one arm like, well, Smarties. Touring the plant, you have to be careful not to step on the moving rubber roadway or you could end up back outside again.

At the centre of the plus sign is a large, open-plan training and fault-rectification area where we parked our black Smart. Trolleyloads of replacement panel sets like Airfix model components were wheeled out for my consideration. It's a bit like buying a new pair of shoes, really. It occurred to me that the Smart would be a great car to buy in kit form since, like Camelot in *Monty Python and the Holy Grail*, it's only a model.

I quite liked the red panels, but then realised that the thick strut that would be the B pillar if the Smart were a complete car would always be black, as it's part of the Tridion safety frame that forms the rigid core of the thing. Didn't really go, so I sent those away.

Silver was quite nice too, but having gone all that way I fancied something a bit more radical. Eventually, realising that it wasn't my car anyway, I selected something called Numeric Blue. The raffishly named and immensely patient Gerard Frangart and Raphaël Marques shouldered me aside, went at the Smart with power tools and fists and, not much more than 30 minutes later, we had something in pale blue and plastered with random numbers. Absurd, really, because the V5 registration document still says it's black.

Within a few miles of beginning the return journey I began to suspect that the whole thing was a terrible mistake. Confirmation came at a roadside burger van, whose proprietor was careful to establish that we worked for a good manly car magazine before agreeing to a photograph of his premises with the gaily coloured Smart in the foreground. Then, prophetically, we got a puncture and were shafted by the owner of a small rural garage.

The Smart's funky enough as it is. A true eccentric doesn't need a silly hat to be recognised as one, and the Smart was enough of a novelty item in plain black. It's a bad comedian who laughs at his own joke, after all. I also began to worry about how the *Top Gear* staff would take it. They went home for the weekend leaving a black Smart parked outside and would return to discover that a conceptual artist had been at it with a tin of psychedelic alphabet soup. I quickly arranged for the original panels to be shipped home as well, just in case.

The Smart, in the end, doesn't need to make a statement. It's convincing enough as a car. In fact, I think I might buy one, because, on returning home, I discovered another advantage of extreme shortness.

The back half of my garage is full of the usual stiff paint brushes, broken bicycles, wellington boots, unidentified tinned substances and 'useful' offcuts of wood. Buying just the front half of a car is going to be a lot easier than clearing all that stuff out.

And they do it in a very nice dark-blue colour.

SOURCES

Car Magazine
'I've never felt such a spanner' (July 1997); 'If he knows, he's not saying anything' (August 1996); 'Police car, lights, action' (May 1998); 'Don't forget your toolkit' (June 1995); 'The Vauxhall Vectra, a representative view' (August 1995); 'The Motown Story' (January 1998).

Top Gear
'How great cars come to be abandoned in old barns' (September 2006); 'Some observations on rear-end handling' (January 2005); 'These modern supercars are all bloody rubbish you know' (December 2005); 'Brown's green tax – a bit of a grey area' (March 2005); 'It's a car, Jimmy, but not as we know it' (April 2006); 'How the peace and quiet of England was ruined by the noise of people complaining' (June 2006); 'Jeremy Clarkson ruined my dream car' (August

2006); 'Is it a car? Is it a bike? No. And no.' (March 2000); 'A clot on the landscape' (April 2001); 'I'm just going to Iceland. I may be some time.' (December 2001); 'Harley-Davidson, a hanging offence' (October 2001); 'The Smart car. Not after we'd finished with it.' (July 2002); 'Charles Darwin may be onto something' (March 2005); 'Achtung! Bentley!' (September 1999).

Daily Telegraph
'This is personal' (March 2006); 'Poetry on motion' (April 2004); 'The best driving song in the world ever' (May 2005); 'This Jaguar looks a bit half-baked to me' (June 2005); 'My cup runneth over and into the centre console' (January 2004); 'Track days, or the futility of going nowhere' (October 2005); 'Be afraid. Be very afraid. But only of the size of the bill.' (October 2005); 'The technical revolution in the toyshop' (November 2005); 'The folly of trying to save fuel' (November 2005); 'Any colour you like, as long as it's available from Dulux' (November 2005); 'Breaking down is not so hard to do' (November 2005); 'The Range Rover of outstanding natural beauty' (December 2005); 'Please keep off the mud' (December 2005); 'How to deal with van drivers' (December 2005); 'Naked motorcycle porn showing now' (January 2006); 'Pious Porsche peddles pathetic pedal-powered product' (January 2006); 'Lamborghinis are great. You should have one.' (February 2006); 'The future of in-car entertainment' (February 2006); 'Porsche outperforms desktop printer shock' (March 2006); 'In case you're reading this on the bog, here are some equations of motion' (May 2006); 'Men, rise up and embrace the wheelbrace'

(May 2006); 'Classic cars – you have been warned' (May 2006); 'I'm gay, but not that gay' (June 2006); 'The building blocks of the car of the future' (June 2006); 'Only the French would build a car designed to break down' (June 2006); 'Britain's surface industry fails to deliver' (July 2006).

Conde Nast Traveller
'A cheap holiday in someone else's camper van misery' (August 2002).

INDEX